# Celebrating Our Call

*Ordination Stories*
*of Presbyterian Women*

EDITED BY

Patricia Lloyd-Sidle

Geneva Press
Louisville, Kentucky

Scripture quotations, unless otherwise indicated, are from the New Revised Standard Version of the Bible, copyright © 1989 by the Division of Christian Education of the National Council of the Churches of Christ in the U.S.A., and used by permission.

See acknowledgments pages 159–60 for additional permission information.

*Book design by Sharon Adams*
*Cover design by Night & Day Design*

*First edition*
Published by Geneva Press
Louisville, Kentucky

This book is printed on acid-free paper that meets the American National Standards Institute Z39.48 standard. ∞

PRINTED IN THE UNITED STATES OF AMERICA

06 07 08 09 10 11 12 13 14 15 — 10 9 8 7 6 5 4 3 2 1

**Library of Congress Cataloging-in-Publication Data**

Celebrating our call : ordination stories of Presbyterian women / [edited by Patricia Lloyd-Sidle].— 1st ed.
　　p. cm.
　ISBN-13: 978-0-664-50287-4 (alk. paper)
　ISBN-10: 0-664-50287-3
　1. Presbyterian Church—United States—Biography. 2. Women—United States—Biography. I. Lloyd-Sidle, Patricia.
　BX9220.C45 2006
　262'.145137082—dc22　　　　　　　　　　　　　　　　　　　　2005054192

# Contents

# Preface

## Patricia Lloyd-Sidle

$K$neeling, feeling the touch of those many hands, I looked up after my grandfather's prayer and saw tears streaming down his face. It was the only time I ever saw him cry.

What depth of gratitude and sorrow did those tears at my ordination service reflect? He was proud of course. Was he also remembering the many women he had accompanied as they struggled to serve God in a church that blocked or belittled them?

Certainly he knew how very fortunate I was to have a family of strong women and loving men, to have wise mentors and multiple role models of women leaders, and to be educated in institutions that encourage women in leadership.

Serving as volume editor for *Celebrating Our Call: Ordination Stories of Presbyterian Women* has been a wonderful way for me to celebrate the twenty-fifth anniversary of my ordination, as well as to join the 2005–2006 triple anniversary celebration: one hundred years of women deacons; seventy-five years of women elders; and fifty years of women ministers.

How grateful I am to the women who shared their stories for this book! Each story is a personal gift, carefully prepared and presented with great love. If you read the book cover to cover you would never guess that these women did not meet or see what each other wrote. Despite representing a wide spectrum of theological beliefs, they share many common experiences as leaders of this denomination. May God bless our reading and receiving.

*2020: year anniversary*
*115 Deacon*
*90 Elders*
*65 minister*

Chapter 1

# "Now Is the Time!"

## An Introduction by Jane Parker Huber

> *Elder Jane Parker Huber has advocated for women in her many leadership roles at all levels of the church. She is the author of many hymns, "fresh words to familiar tunes," several of which are included in* The Presbyterian Hymnal. *Jane has received many honors, including the "Valiant Woman" award by Church Women United.*

*W*hen I was two and a half years old, my mother left me and my older brother and sister. She was only gone for a few days, and I am sure we were left in competent, loving care, but it sounds so dramatic to say, "She left me!" She was off to the General Assembly in 1929 to be one of three young women with the "Committee of 100 Women" gathered to consider a report on the "causes of unrest among women in the Presbyterian Church (U.S.A.)." I do not know how or by whom the three young women were chosen, but there they were: Katharine Sellars, Eleanore Rhind, and my mother, Katharine McAfee Parker. Each was the wife of a man ordained to the ministry of Word and Sacrament, although the three husbands followed different paths: one as a seminary professor (Ovid Sellars, professor of Old Testament at McCormick); one as a pastor (John Rhind); and my father, Albert G. Parker Jr., who was about to move in August 1929 to southern Indiana, called as the president of Presbyterian-related Hanover College in Hanover, Indiana.

These young women were in their early thirties at the time of the 1929 General Assembly in St. Paul, Minnesota, and while their primary activity was child rearing, their thoughts and prayers were also for the good of the church.

They were fascinated by the strong, articulate women in the Committee of 100. They were impressed by the older women's knowledge of and dedication to the church and were persuaded that it was time for women in the church to be ordained to the leadership to which God called them. My mother liked to say that she didn't know exactly why the three young women were invited

Elder Jane Parker Huber (*Courtesy of the author.*)

to be there, but surely one reason was that it made it probable that at least someone would be there fifty years later to tell about it. In 1980 they were all three still alive, and my mother was invited to "tell about it" at the 1980 General Assembly (United Presbyterian Church U.S.A.) women's breakfast in Detroit. On behalf of the 1929 Committee of 100 Women (living and dead) my mother told this story. [1]

On the day before the report was to be presented to the General Assembly, some dignitaries of the church (all men, of course) came to urge them NOT to bring the issue of women's ordination to the Assembly since our Presbyterian Church was in serious talks with the southern Presbyterian Church (PCUS) about reunion and nothing should jeopardize those conversations. (It would be another six decades and more before that reunion would take place.) The women in 1929 said, "NO! Now is the time!"

I am proud to know that my mother was part of that emphatic response. In the year following General Assembly 1929, even though the presbyteries rejected the ordination of women as ministers of the Word, they did approve the ordination of women as elders, and the church is richer for it. Beginning right after the General Assembly in 1930, women elders have brought their gifts of faith and intellect, thoughtfulness and strength, listening and speaking, creativity and perseverance ultimately to every council and committee of the church. It is hard to imagine our church today without the gifts of women serving in leadership alongside men.

The action that successfully initiated the vote on women's ordination was not the only thing that happened at the 1929 General Assembly. One other significant action was the election of my grandfather, Cleland B. McAfee, as moderator. Grandfather McAfee was a healer, a moderator in every sense of the word, a preacher and teacher of systematic and practical theology. He was also the father of three outstanding daughters: in addition to my mother, who ultimately was on the National Council of Presbyterian Women and on the Board of Foreign Missions, there was her older sister, Ruth McAfee Brown; a creative Christian educator and mother of Robert McAfee Brown; and the youngest sister, Mildred McAfee Horton, president of Wellesley College and Captain of the WAVES during World War II.

In 1929–30 the church was in the midst of one of its great arguments between fundamentalists and literalists, on one side, and, on the other, modernists and those willing to accept change as God led them. My grandfather stood firmly with the latter while still loving those determined not to budge an inch. Throughout the year of criss-crossing the country, this pastor/preacher/teacher spoke healing words of love and inclusiveness that surely must have been a factor in the presbyteries' votes and positive conviction not only about women's ordination as elders but other issues as well. My grandfather died in 1944 more than a decade before women could be ordained to the ministry of Word and Sacrament. I honor his gift to our generation proudly, even knowing that he did not live long enough to see and adopt all the changes that have taken place in the intervening years and that he would have supported.

What are some of the issues and changes of recent decades that receive greater attention because there are significant numbers of women in church leadership?

- Inclusive language in worship and in printed materials
- Racism as it particularly affects women
- Women's issues, which often have a different "slant" when considered by both men and women, such as
  - sexual harassment in the church
  - rape and sexual abuse in the home
  - problem pregnancy and contraception

Economic justice for women became an issue and several informative and awareness-raising conferences were planned in the Washington, DC area where the concerns could be brought quickly to Congress. Attention was also called to economic justice for women in the church. While men and women were equally commissioned as missionaries, their salaries were not equal. And it seemed to be assumed that church secretaries, for example, held their jobs simply "because they loved the Lord and the church."

Before we get too far away from the issue of women and racism, some clarification is in order. Women had achieved one goal with gaining the right to ordination. Working through that particular inequality meant that they began to understand something about inequality in general, but it did not mean that inequality in one area was the same as inequality in another. Coming to a deeper understanding requires time, patience, and a lot of hard work. I have a picture in my mind of a meeting of COWAC (the Council on Women and the Church) when I chaired that council. The room was as nondescript as such meeting rooms usually are, windowless and fairly crowded. I looked around at the large circle of beautiful faces and realized that there were more other-than-white faces than plain-old-white faces looking back at me. They were all sizes, shapes, ages, inclinations, convictions—it was a breath-taking sight! A baby step, but even tiny steps were significant.

One big "for example" in my life of how women's leadership has opened windows to other issues in the church is the importance of inclusive language in our worship of God. When we were working on planning the program for the United Presbyterian Women's National Meeting in 1976, we were determined to use inclusive language as a way of introducing (or reinforcing) its use to women from across the country and around the world. Among other factors, we were looking for a hymn that would fit the theme and the Bible study (Luke 4, especially verses 16 through 21). When we didn't find such a hymn, I wrote one, thus starting a lifelong avocation.

So that the hymn would be easy to sing, I used a standard, familiar hymn tune in a well-known meter in public domain. That was a fortunate decision because it blended the "old music" (Truro, Thomas Williams, 1789) with the "new words" ("Live into Hope," Jane Parker Huber, 1976), ensuring ease in learning the new hymn and opening the door to many familiar tunes in public domain but with new words in contemporary language.

> Live into hope of captives freed, of sight regained, the end of greed.
>     Th'oppressed shall be the first to see the year of God's own jubilee!
> Live into hope the blind shall see with insight and with clarity,
>     Removing shades of pride and fear—a vision of our God brought near.
> Live into hope of liberty, the right to speak, the right to be,
>     The right to have one's daily bread, to hear God's word and thus be fed.
> Live into hope of captives freed from chains of fear or want or greed.
>     God now proclaims our full release to faith and hope and joy
>         and peace.

It was a time when people were beginning to realize that there were many ideas alive in the church but without expression in hymnody. In the next few decades a flood of new hymns appeared, some with new music and many set to familiar tunes.

Ordination was not required for women to find ways to respond to God's call. The "church work" that women had found to do or created for themselves tended to be focused on mission causes in the years before ordination was won. In the earliest years of "women's work" in the early 1800s, women were active wherever they saw need. They helped supply suitable clothing for seminary students. They fed and clothed the needy. They visited the sick and lonely. They also recognized their own spiritual needs, so they prayed, studied the Bible, and shared their lives, enacting in their own ways the priesthood of all believers as they ministered to each other.

Many women found places to exercise their gifts through mission work when opportunities did not exist at home. Women missionaries could be doctors in other countries before they were welcomed as doctors in this country. There were also careers in education in other countries that were more open to women.

Women formed their own organizations and mission societies, working without the benefit of staff, carrying on all correspondence by hand, endeavoring to fill the gaps in denominational mission. They were concerned especially about work with the health and education of women and children in this country and around the world. They kept in close personal touch especially with single-women missionaries. They were aware of the loneliness and even danger that was often characteristic of the mission field, particularly for women alone in an unfamiliar land and culture. One major cause for unrest in the 1920s was that the women's mission boards had been absorbed into the denomination's boards, thus taking away the control and independence that had been built up over the years.

Once ordination as elders was approved for women, there were still some rough spots along the road to full acceptance. It was, after all, up to a congregation to decide to elect and ordain women. As late as the 1983 reunion of Presbyterians there were still some congregations that refused to ordain women.

There were also happy moments along the way. I recall my mother's excitement as they were planning the Presbyterian Women's National Meeting in Grand Rapids in 1946 when there were enough women elders to serve communion. Until that time they had always had to depend on male elders and pastors to serve the sacrament. That was also the meeting attended by the Rev. Mrs. Tamaki Uemura, the first Japanese civilian to be invited to this country after the war and allowed to enter the United States. A request that she be permitted to administer the sacrament at the meeting caused great consternation and intense debate and was refused.

At the 181st General Assembly of the United Presbyterian Church U.S.A. in May 1969, a significant report came from a Special Committee on the Status of Women in Church and Society, recommending the use of inclusive language for the people of God and the establishment of a permanent Council on Women and the Church. People who were present recall how the report was received with laughter from those opposed to its ideas. In all probability there were some people muttering under their breath, "I've been saying it would come to this!" Ultimately perhaps the laughter and scorn helped make it clear that women's issues were real, but the hurt was real too.

There was often particular reluctance to ordain the pastor's wife as an elder even if her skills and interests made her well qualified for leadership. For decades there were certain expectations, unwritten but implied and imposed on "the minister's wife"—to be honest, it is still true in some quarters today. Many of us can remember a time when she was expected to teach Sunday school. It was often considered a flaw if she couldn't play the piano or direct a children's choir. In spite of unfair expectations and equally unfair limitations, clergy spouses, and other women as well, served the church in a multitude of ways: washing and ironing communion linens; preparing, serving, and organizing meals for bereaved families and others in need; cleaning the church kitchen; providing child care; volunteering in Christian education. The list was endless.

When my husband was in seminary (1948–1951) at least one professor stated that it would be "inappropriate" for a pastor's wife to be an elder. That attitude deterred church nominating committees for about twenty-five years! Interestingly, once women could be ordained to the ministry of Word and Sacrament, it seemed perfectly obvious that the husband of a minister was eligible for ordination as an elder!

There is an obvious fact to keep in mind: *The original votes to include women in ordained ministry were made entirely by men.* They had to be! Picture in your mind's eye every General Assembly, synod, and presbytery meeting made up entirely of men in black suits and white shirts. We are much more colorful today—in many ways! Some of us can remember when the proper form of address in beginning to speak at such a meeting was "Fathers and Brethren." This was true even a quarter century after women could be ordained as elders and the question being debated was whether women could be ordained to the ministry of Word and Sacrament. Although there were usually a few women elder commissioners to the various assemblies of the church, there were never enough women for a decisive swing vote. I remember with special fondness and gratitude the men who could so clearly see and articulate the importance of including women in leadership and who worked diligently along with women on women's behalf.

Here we are in 2005–2006 celebrating one hundred years of women's ordination as deacons, seventy-five years of women's ordination as elders, and fifty years as ministers of Word and Sacrament. How clever was it to achieve these three milestones of women's ordination about a quarter century apart so they could (and would!) be celebrated at the same time? On the other hand, the quarter-century gaps indicate that it takes a whole generation to make much progress.

By 1971, at the 183rd General Assembly in Rochester, New York, Lois Stair had been elected the first woman moderator of the United Presbyterian Church U.S.A., proving by her style and competence that women were ready. In 1978, at the 118th Presbyterian Church U.S. General Assembly in Shreveport, Louisiana, five years before Presbyterian reunion, Sara Bernice Mosely was elected the first woman moderator in the PCUS; then following reunion in 1983, she served as the first Moderator of the General Assembly Council. The southern church had waited longer to ordain women, but when they did, ordination was for both elders and ministers of the Word.

When we gathered in Syracuse twenty-five years ago, there was a strong sense of the Spirit's presence as we celebrated those earlier milestones of fifty and twenty-five years, of elders and ministers of the Word and Sacrament, respectively. Our numbers were so much more significant than they had been in the very early years of testing the reality and the acceptance of women's ordination to leadership roles in the church. The Syracuse gathering proved that although the journey was difficult, we were moving ahead. I will always be grateful to Gail Ricciuti for her sermon about the Hebrew midwives, Shiphrah and Puah—with new insights and new appreciation for the strength of women.

As you read the chapters in this book, each one recounting the experiences and reflections of a particular woman, be grateful to God for each person. With you, they make the story complete. I count it a very special blessing to have lived through these seventy-five years since women could first be ordained as elders. I long ago graduated from hats and gloves and no longer worry about what to wear serving communion. Two daughters, a son, and a granddaughter are elders along with me. We stand at the start of a new century with new doors to open, new mountains to climb. Thank God for the mountains and the climbing and those who climb with us!

Chapter 2

# Generation to Generation

## Joanna M. Adams

*Joanna Adams is known for building bridges of understanding in both the community and in the church. She has served five Presbyterian congregations and is nationally recognized for her preaching and writing skills. She and her husband of forty years, attorney Alfred B. Adams, have a daughter, a son, and two grandchildren.*

$W$hen I was a girl, my most beloved make-believe game involved preaching to my dolls. I would line them up on my bed, turn the radio on so that no one outside my room, especially my brother, could hear me, and deliver heart-felt sermons to them. What joy! They listened in rapt attention to every word, not a single one ever blinking an eye. What is striking to me in retrospect is that I had never heard a woman preach and would do so only after I had begun my seminary studies a couple of decades later. In 1957, playing preacher could have been comparable to envisioning oneself as an astronaut before the Russians sent Sputnik, the first satellite, into space. Very few little girls in Mississippi in the 1950s could have imagined themselves as ministers. There was no such thing in our reality. For me, playing preacher was simply a pleasurable way to wile away an afternoon. Not until I was grown did I realize that, even before my birth, I was being drawn toward ministry as filings are drawn toward a magnet.

My mother and father named me after my mother's parents—Anna and John. Both died long before I was born, my grandfather passing away under dramatic circumstances when my mother was a child. Papa, as she called him, had been a preacher in south Georgia. According to family lore, he was possessed of a quick wit and a heart as wide as the marshes of Glynn. The family did not have an abundance of material resources, given the fact that there were five growing children and one small-town preacher's salary. But parishioners supplemented these resources with baskets of fresh vegetables and chickens that my mother wanted to turn into pets but were destined for the dinner table.

One Sunday afternoon, my grandfather kissed his family good-bye and went off to preach the evening service in Waycross, Georgia. His sermon text that night was the final verse of the fifteenth chapter of 1 Corinthians, a magnificent excursus by Paul on the meaning of Jesus' resurrection and the resurrection of the dead. For fifty-six verses, Paul soars to great theological heights: "Listen, I will tell you a mystery! We will not all die, but we will all be changed, in a moment, in the twinkling of an eye, at the last trumpet. For the trumpet will sound, and the dead will be raised imperishable. . . . The sting of death is sin, and the power of sin is the law. But thanks be to God, who gives us the victory through our Lord Jesus Christ" (1 Cor. 15: 51–52, 56–57). Then comes the reentry into the earth's atmosphere: "Therefore, my beloved, be steadfast, immovable, always excelling in the work of the Lord, because you know that in the Lord your labor is not in vain" (v. 58). In the middle of the sermon, my grandfather collapsed to the floor. He had suffered a cerebral hemorrhage that took his life two days later.

As a child, I loved to think about this grandfather whom I never knew. Not his death but his life and ministry. I was especially taken with the story of the day my mother was playing with her dolls in the front parlor. The year was some time between 1915 and 1920. She heard a noise in the closet in the front hall and went to take a look. When she opened the door, she discovered a man, an African American, hiding there. She screamed and ran to the kitchen where her mother was. "Don't be afraid, Helen," my grandmother said. "The man in the closet is a friend of your father. Some people in town think that he has stolen something, but he hasn't. Papa is waiting until the sun goes down, and then he's going to help him slip out of town and not be harmed."

Though I grew up in the segregated South, with its "white" and "colored" water fountains and other more menacing forms of prejudice, I was also shaped by other forces, such as a legacy of compassion for all people, especially the marginalized and the excluded, from my grandfather John and my grandmother Anna.

I believe that my mother would have herself been a wonderful minister, but that was an option she could not and would not have ever considered. She was a person of her time, as are we all. She was a high school teacher of Latin and French. She loved literature and language, her husband, and her children. She took in sick relatives and would stop the car in the middle of traffic to remove a turtle from the center of the road. After my first Easter sermon, she said to me, "Jo, I can tell you believe in the resurrection. That's the main thing, and you helped us all today." What a gift those words were to me.

I am grateful that I have been able to claim a rich family legacy of ministry, and I am not the first woman to do so. My mother's sister, my aunt "Squeaky" as I called her, was the Christian educator at our church when I was growing up. It was from her that I learned the most important lesson I have ever learned about the grace of God. One Saturday morning, Squeaky gave me permission to go on an exploration expedition around the church while she finished up some work at her desk. I was staying with her for the weekend, and things had gotten a little boring already. She was into vegetable soup and going to bed early. I was not.

What a time I had, wandering wherever I wanted in that big and mysterious place that was our church. I stood behind the pulpit and pretended. I poked around the room where Mr. Porter rehearsed the choir every Wednesday evening. Finally, I came to a door that was closed. Of course, it had to be opened. I tried the knob. It turned. I entered and encountered a heavenly sight: mountains of snowy white bread cubes, plied high on shining silver plates; towers of silver trays filled, I discovered, with tiny glass cups brimming with grape juice. I had come upon the little kitchen near the sanctuary where the women of the church prepared the elements for Sunday communion.

All of a sudden, I was overcome with the feeling of being famished. I had to have just one little cube of bread. I took a piece and ate it. It was not enough. I ate another one and another, and then I was grabbing communion bread by the handful and stuffing it in my mouth, which naturally made me thirsty, so I drank one thimble-full of grape juice and then another and another, and so it went until I looked up and saw my aunt Squeaky standing at the door. I could not hide my purple mustache. "I'm sorry," I said.

"I accept your apology," she said. "Let's wash the cups and cut some more bread." It was the most grace-filled moment of my life. I never say the words of institution at the Lord's Table without remembering that the purpose of Christ's sacrifice was not punishment but redemption.

As the young wife of a busy attorney and a young mother in my early twenties, I found myself teaching an adult Sunday school at our neighborhood Presbyterian church. The topic was "Faith and Feminism." A woman whom I greatly admired, a college professor and mother of four, had called and asked me to do it, and I was not nimble enough on the telephone to come up with a reason why not, other than that I knew very little about either subject, a reservation that she put into perspective by saying, "You'll learn."

It was the early 1970s, a time of great transition for women, both in the church and in society. Betty Friedan's *The Feminine Mystique,* published in 1963, had finally made it to the South, and its impact was profound. So was the resistance. It was wonderful to be part of a congregation in which the gifts of women were considered a blessing and not a threat.

It was life changing to worship with a community in which equality for all people, social justice, and war and peace were talked about as basic matters of faith. Not only did I teach the Faith and Feminism class, I led a women's circle, preparing both the brownies and the Bible study on a regular basis. I also helped out with a day-care program sponsored by our church in a nearby public housing project. It was unsettling to realize the paucity of resources and opportunities that were available for the boys and girls I came to know and love and who were my neighbors.

One day, I was sitting at the lunch table with four of my little friends. I was trying to get them to eat their vegetables. "Those peas on your plate are delicious," I said. "You should try them." "What are peas?" one of the children asked me. None of the rest knew either. My eyes were opened that day to the two worlds that are the United States of America. At home I was reading to my five-year-old from *The Chronicles of Narnia,* and here were kids, just as precious in the eyes of God as my own, who didn't know what peas were.

My church was teaching me that to be a follower of Christ was to move more deeply into the lives and needs of my neighbor. The door of my heart was opening. One November, our family was asked to expand our Thanksgiving table to host international guests. That day I learned that to be a member of the household of God was to be a friend to the world. To this day, I pray for Mr. Ossman, Mr. Albersan, and Mr. Harun, the three Muslim men who were our guests.

Over time, I have moved from the understanding of God that had been molded primarily by the pietistic tradition of my childhood, with its emphasis on personal salvation, to an awareness of God that encompasses both personal faith and the broader realms of society and culture. I became aware that the church of Jesus Christ could not limit its concerns to church affairs, because God is involved in more than ecclesiastical matters. I vividly remember hearing a benediction at the close of the service one Sunday in which our pastor reminded us that God did not live in the sanctuary during the week but lived in the world where people suffered and longed for freedom and dignity, justice and compassion. I wept all the way home. I had heard the gospel.

Before long, I was yearning to learn more about the Bible and theology. Should I go to seminary? When I broached the subject with my husband, I was heartened by his response: "I always knew you were going to do something interesting, which is one of the reasons I married you. I knew I would never be bored!"

Many people thought I had lost my mind. Women like me did not do what I was setting out to do. Though the South was changing, the socially acceptable vocational roles for women were still homemaking, teaching, and nursing. I had a call from God to be a wife and mother, but I was beginning to sense that there was something more I was being called to do. The crucial question when I began seminary is the same question I have wrestled with every day since my ordination: How can I hold together the different commitments of my life, each of which is profoundly important to me? The answer has been a work in progress, with different emphases at different times, depending on family needs and church demands.

On a practical level, I still find holidays to be daunting. I remember the year I preached the Thanksgiving Day sermon at the church in the morning and in the early afternoon served Thanksgiving dinner, which I had prepared, complete with ambrosia and pumpkin pie with fresh whipped cream for dessert. It has been hard to let go of various parts of my life when they come into conflict because I love them all.

When I began my studies at Columbia Theological Seminary, I did so with a hunger to learn in my soul, though I was terrified by the notion of being a preacher or pastor. "I want to take only Bible and theology courses, please," I said to the Dean. Since I was entering as a part-time student, I was allowed to begin under those conditions, but before the first semester was over, I realized that something significant within me was coming to life. The Latin word *vocare* means "to call." My call was emerging in the passion with which I studied and engaged in dialogue with professors and fellow students. My first Bible course was on the Elijah and Elisha stories in 1 and 2 Kings. The teacher was a visiting Scotsman who made the ancient texts leap to life. I felt as if I had died and gone to heaven.

Catherine González, Professor of Church History, was the only female faculty member when I began at Columbia. She was the first woman I heard preach a sermon. She was gracious enough to gather the women students under her wing and made sure we knew the history of how the church had treated women across the centuries. It was not a pretty picture, but she modeled for me how important it was "not to let the sun set on your anger" but to use your gifts to build up the church and help correct its course. There are plenty of things to be angry and frustrated about, but the church has also been the most affirming, generative institution in my life.

To be sure, Paul said that women should keep silent in church, but he was not making a universal pronouncement for all time. Instead, he was responding to a particular problem in a particular situation. I find great joy in the fact that in the Gospels the women who followed Jesus were the first witnesses and testifiers to the resurrection. One of them was named Joanna. If the women had been silent, there would have been no glad tidings to pass from generation to generation.

At seminary, there was a group of male students who were uncomfortable with the presence of female students on campus. One day a fellow in the group said to me, "Joanna, we pray every day that you will see the light." He ended up dropping out of seminary, and I graduated with honors. I also received the Florrie Wilkes Sanders Theology Prize. Ms. Sanders was an Atlanta matriarch and intellectual with a keen interest in theology. In the 1920s she had gone up to New Haven to attend Yale Divinity School. The professors had insisted that she sit in the back of the lecture hall so that she would not distract "the real students." When I was called to my first church as head of staff, Ms. Sanders's daughter, Sylvia Sanders Kelley, brought me as a gift a framed quotation by Antoinette Brown, the first woman to be ordained to the Christian ministry in the United States. Her remarks were made at the World Parliament of Religions in Chicago, 1893: Women are needed in the pulpit as imperatively and for the same reason they are needed in the world—because they are women. Women have become— or when the ingrained habit of unconscious imitation has been superseded—they will become indispensable to the religious evolution of the human race.

Throughout my ministry, I have stayed close to the seminary, supporting it in every way I could, including chairing the Board of Trustees and serving on several significant search committees. The school shaped and formed me and made me fit to serve Christ and his church. It was my spiritual mother. By graduation, I had come to the place where I could claim the vocation for which I was made and into which I continue to grow.

In 1979, I was ordained to the ministry of Word and Sacrament at Central Presbyterian church in downtown Atlanta, where I served for the next seven years as associate pastor and minister to the community. At the time, I was the only woman serving full-time in a parish position in Atlanta Presbytery.

I led worship for the first time at Central on Pentecost Sunday. After church, there was a reception for my family and me in the fellowship hall. It was a lovely party, with cucumber sandwiches cut in triangles and lime sherbet punch. I wore a red dress in celebration of the gift of the Holy Spirit to the early church.

As I stood in the receiving line, one of the elders of the church tapped me on the shoulder. "There are some people here to see you," he said. I looked in the direction he was pointing and saw two people who were obviously in distress. They looked disheveled and anxious. I remember wishing that they had waited until the party was over. I walked over to ask them what they needed. It turned out that they needed just about everything. They were hungry and homeless, a situation complicated by their mental disabilities. I spent the afternoon trying to find a place for them to stay and was horrified to realize

Joanna M. Adams invites her congregation at Morningside Presbyterian Church in Atlanta to the Lord's Table. (*Courtesy of the author.*)

that there was literally no place that they could stay together in the entire city. From that afternoon on, Jesus kept showing up at our door in the form of the stranger. It changed our church forever. The night shelter we began in the church gym was the first one downtown, and from it, literally dozens of shelters and feeding programs were born, along with strong, collaborative advocacy work that continues today. My entire ministry has been shaped by my encounter with two guests who showed up uninvited to the party on Pentecost. I am convinced that God sent them.

Since my ordination, I have always served as a parish pastor. Over the years, I have been called to five congregations in five different contexts and at different points in their histories, but they have all had in common the centrality of worship and a strong commitment to imaginative, creative involvement with the community and the world. Their taproots go down deep into the gospel of Jesus Christ, from whom their identity, strength, and mission are derived.

I love most things about being a parish pastor and am usually able to tolerate the things I don't love, such as wedding photographers with an attitude and people who yawn in church. I can handle a small yawn with the hand politely covering the mouth; it is when I can count the crowns on the back molars that I get annoyed. Even after all these years, I still experience disrespect sometimes. Not long ago after church, someone said to me, "You are the first woman I have heard preach. You weren't bad, and your voice didn't grate on my nerves, as women's voices usually do." Did he consider that a compliment?

Then there was the father of the bride who said to me after the ceremony, "When Nancy and Bob come to see us after the honeymoon, we're going to get our minister to say a few words over them. We're not sure it really takes if a woman says them." That evolution of the human race of which Antoinette Brown spoke can't come soon enough for me.

Among the most satisfying aspects of ministry for me has been helping congregations revitalize and discover the future God has in mind for them. I also love evangelism and have been privileged to serve several churches that grew significantly, both in numbers and in spiritual maturity while I was their pastor. I love to help people wrestle with the great social and ethical issues of our time, using the resources of our faith tradition. I love to teach the Bible and have led women's Bible studies in every church I have served. I find great satisfaction in being a pastor and feel blessed when people allow me to walk through the heights and depths of life with them, serving as a vessel for the presence and power of God.

I have been active in ecumenical, Jewish/Christian, and interfaith work over the years and have found the friendships I made in those endeavors to be as precious as those I share with Presbyterian colleagues. For me, to follow Christ is to follow him into relationship with members of God's richly diverse human family. I believe that Christ is the way to salvation, and because I believe it, I try to follow his way of compassion and peace and respect for basic human dignity.

The ministry of preaching is central to my life and vocation. Last summer, I celebrated the twenty-fifth year of my ordination as a Presbyterian minister. The anniversary came at an odd time. For the first time in a quarter of a century, I was not preaching or leading worship on Sunday mornings on a regular basis. On one level it was a relief not to be worrying about next week's sermon while I brushed my teeth, scrambled an egg, or watched a movie. "Is there anything more unrelenting than the task of preaching?" I asked myself. "No," I assured myself. Well, maybe labor pains before the birth of quintuplets.

I told myself that it might be time to seek a less-demanding ministry, one that didn't require the sacrifice of Saturday nights out with my husband or cause me routinely to question whether I would ever have anything meaningful to say to anybody again. Forget preaching, a little voice in my head kept admonishing, but in the end I couldn't do it. How could I forget the indescribable gladness that comes from those moments in the pulpit when I sense that I have been a genuine vessel of divine grace? How could I walk away from the power of the story of creation and redemption that has been entrusted to the church and passed on from generation to generation? How could I walk away from the privilege of proclaiming the enduring Word during my fleeting little moment on this earth?

In the end, I could not forget preaching. Being the bearer of Good News turned out to be an irresistible occupation for me. Back in the pulpit, I am naturally encountering the same daunting realities I have faced since the day I knelt down on the sanctuary floor, had hands laid upon me, and received the peculiar office to which I have been called. I wouldn't trade my vocation as preacher for anything, but there are some things I wish I had known when I went into this line of work originally, the most important of which is that preaching isn't easy. Truth is difficult to discover. Sentences are hard to craft. Effective public speaking requires disciplined commitment. Handling the responsibility of being "servants of Christ and stewards of God's mysteries" (1 Cor. 4:1) is not for the faint of heart.

But then, nothing that has staying power or that offers a genuinely new life ever comes easily. Every week I pray. Every week I study. Every once in a blue moon, the sermon comes easily, but most weeks I labor. I stare at the computer screen. I chew my pencil eraser. I become convinced that this is the week I have been dreading all along: there will be no Word from the Lord, and I might as well go ahead and jump out the window. Then, the miracle. The Spirit breaks through with a light that shows me the way home to God. I discover, once again, that we preach, as we live, by grace. I trust the power of the Word. "Preacher" is not the easiest vocation in the world, but I cannot imagine a richer or more meaningful one.

I have faced a few challenges since my ordination. I have been a steady voice for the inclusion of all people whom God calls to ordained service in the church, and that has often put me in the line of fire. When I was called to my longest and most exciting pastorate, at Trinity Presbyterian Church in Atlanta, I followed a much-beloved founding pastor who had retired after a forty-one year tenure. I tried a brave experiment in coleadership for a couple of years in Chicago, which effectively meant that my husband and I had to deal with a two-city marriage. Now I am enjoying serving a congregation that is small in size but growing every Sunday. Though the church has had a number of obstacles to overcome in recent years, it has become mighty in faith and hope.

On winter Sundays, I turn on the boiler in the church basement. In the fall, I sweep the leaves off the sidewalk. I am blessed to be a part of a community that is open to the fresh wind of the Spirit and believes that through God's grace, all things are still possible. For many years, I relished the complexity and challenge of leadership on a large scale in large churches, but now I am in a different place. I am learning all over again the meaning of my favorite parable, which begins, "The kingdom of God is like a mustard seed" (Mark 4:30–32). The longer I live into my ordination, the more I relate to the wisdom of Qohelet: "For everything there is a season, and a time for every purpose under heaven" (Eccl. 3:1).

A wise friend once said, "You cannot prove the promises of God in advance, but if you live them, they turn out to be true every time." That has been the story of my life and ministry. I keep a photograph of my grandfather John and my grandmother Anna in my study. Often, I look at them with love and gratitude. I trust the feeling is mutual.

Chapter 3

# Wearing the Robe

## Deborah A. Block

*Deborah Block is pastor and head of staff at Immanuel Presbyterian Church in Milwaukee, a congregation she has served since she was ordained in 1977. She serves the larger church and community in many capacities, including as moderator of Milwaukee Presbytery and member of the boards of Carroll College, McCormick Seminary, and the Presbyterian Publishing Corporation.*

"As God's chosen ones, holy and beloved, clothe yourselves with compassion, kindness, humility, meekness, and patience. Bear with one another and, if anyone has a complaint against another, forgive each other; just as the Lord has forgiven you, so you must also forgive. Above all, clothe yourselves with love, which binds everything together in perfect harmony. And let the peace of Christ rule in your hearts, to which indeed you were called in the one body. And be thankful."

(Col. 3:12–16)

*H*oping to be the chosen one—holy and beloved didn't matter that much— I clothed myself in my white robe and went to preach my audition sermon for the associate pastor nominating committee from Immanuel Presbyterian Church in Milwaukee. It was the fall of 1977. Working down that list,

I was *humbled* by the opportunity to be considered by this august, and as I recall, rather austere committee.

I was *impatient*. This was only my second interview in seven months, after an unforgiving three years of seminary, one of four women in my class. I was sure that God was calling me, but no one else seemed to have my number. In the time between the times, I was working at my alma mater, Carroll College, as a head resident in one of the dorms, for room and board.

The *peace of Christ* was not ruling in my heart, and I was just hoping the *word of Christ* might dwell in me enough to preach a passable sermon.

19

Deborah A. Block celebrates baptism at Immanuel Presbyterian Church in Milwaukee. (*Photo taken by Melanie Sikma, courtesy of the author.*)

I had been *admonished* not to do this, for reasons ranging from unbiblical to impractical to unprecedented. The college chaplain had refused to write a letter of recommendation for seminary and urged a consideration of Christian education. The seminary president had called women in ministry "a passing fad." The Presbyterian Church, then twenty years into allowing the ordination of women to ministry, was debating whether it could be optional.

So I went, on the appointed Sunday to the designated pulpit, wearing all of that and my white robe, and sat self-consciously on a too-large chancel chair. There was no market then for liturgical vestments for women, so we made our own. And taking the apostle Paul seriously, we clothed ourselves with the white robes of the early Christian baptismal ritual. A literal and visual "putting on" of the new humanity in Christ, where "all . . . are one in Christ Jesus" (Gal. 3:28).

So they came, on the appointed Sunday to the designated church, wearing dark suits and sitting conspicuously in the back pew. The pastor of Bethany Presbyterian Church introduced me and announced to the congregation that I was preaching for a nominating committee in the area. It was no secret who those guests were, in that small church, or where they were from or what they were doing there. Too much information had already been shared, but there was more from this kindly older minister. Wasn't it wonderful that I had gone to Sunday school right across the hall? Wasn't it special that my grandmother and parents had been members there? Wouldn't they be proud this morning? And then, turning me by the shoulders to the congregation, "Doesn't she look just like a little angel?"

So much for early Christian baptismal imagery—and for any sophistication and composure I had mustered for this crucial moment. I was young (twenty-four) and short (five feet, two inches), and I felt diminutive, diminished, and "little." My face was as red as my robe was white. My thoughts were not angelic.

Suddenly older and wiser, I subsequently decided to clothe myself in the basic black of the Geneva gown. It was a serious look and a serious symbol. As ordination became a reality I was grateful to wear a tradition that, despite opposition, had taken seriously and faithfully the teachings of Jesus and Paul; the witness of Mary, of Mary and Martha, and of Mary Magdalene and Joanna; the ministry of Tabitha, Lydia, Priscilla; and all the unnamed rest—a tradition that now confessionally affirms that the Holy Spirit "calls women and men to all ministries of the Church."

But we confess, too, that it was not always so among us Presbyterians.

Prohibition was not over until May of 1930. In the same month that the Supreme Court of the United States ruled that buying liquor did not violate the Constitution, the General Assembly of the Presbyterian Church voted that ordaining women as elders did not violate the Bible. New wine, fresh wineskins! On June 6, 1930, the Presbyterian Church in Wauwatosa, Wisconsin ordained Miss Sarah E. Dickson to the office of elder, the first woman to hold that office in the Presbyterian Church.

But not many lifted a glass to the lifting of that prohibition. Overture B, which made women eligible for ordination as elders, "was received with only feeble applause" by the Assembly, it was reported. An overture allowing the ordination of women to the ministry lost almost two to one and would not pass for another twenty-six years.

The 1930 decision was a long time in coming. The motion to amend the church's constitution had failed in 1920, the same year the nineteenth amendment to the U.S. Constitution passed, giving women the right to vote. Two Presbyterian women wrote a paper on the "Causes of Unrest Among Women in the Presbyterian Church." "In the interests of 'the peace, purity, unity and progress of the church'" fifteen Presbyterian men were charged with investigating this "dissatisfaction" of women in the church and discovered (!) that women regarded as "unjust [their] lack of representation." A 1929 conference of one hundred women —held in St. Paul, appropriately—resolved "that the church can best be served by making it possible for all the members of the church to find their place of service without other discrimination than ability and capacity." The next year women were given their place as elders.[1]

Practice often follows policy slowly and reluctantly. Doors open, and few are invited to come in to take their place. Women were at the center of mission and education in the church but were not readily invited to move from serving at the kitchen and classroom tables to serving at communion and conference tables.

Enter Lilian Hart Alexander. The only woman at the table when the nominating committee of her church met to discuss new elders, she challenged her colleagues to nominate women to serve on the all-male session of Third Presbyterian Church in Rochester, New York. That accomplished, this suffragette and mother of five turned her attention to the ordination of women to the ministry of the Word. In 1952, the same year that I was born, Mrs. Alexander was gestating an overture to open that door. Arguing that Christianity had been a "potent force in elevating the position of women," her overture claimed that "when a woman is led of God . . . to dedicate her life [to the demands of parish ministry], it would be difficult to discover truly Christian grounds to deny her request for ordination." Citing the emerging leadership of women in society, she named what "is indeed anomalous": "in our church [women] cannot be ordained to preach the gospel." Recalling the "whole emphasis" of Christian tradition, she enjoined, "Let us follow the spirit of our Master and open the doors of His ministry to all." The session of Third Presbyterian Church readily adopted the overture in early 1953, as did the Presbytery of Rochester. In 1956, the approval of Lilian Alexander's overture by the General Assembly gave birth to a new day in the Presbyterian Church. Women *could* be ordained to preach the gospel. The Form of Government was amended to read, "Both men and women may be called to this office."[2]

Enter Margaret Ellen Towner, the first woman to be ordained to the ministry of the Word in the Presbyterian Church (U.S.A.). She was encouraged to initiate the process by Dr. William H. McConaghy, the pastor of her home church in Syracuse, New York. Margaret recalls his letter of June 22, 1956, suggesting that she consider ordination. "He felt the sooner action was taken to bring the denomination along in attitude and procedure the better it would be for the Presbyterian Church." Margaret had earned a B.D. at Union Theological Seminary in New York City and was a commissioned church worker serving as the director of Christian education at the First Presbyterian Church of Allentown, Pennsylvania. The plan was to transfer her back to the Presbytery of Cayuga-Syracuse for ordination, a process followed carefully and in consultation with the stated clerk of the General Assembly, Dr. Eugene Carson Blake, to ensure that all was done decently and in order. A service for ordination was scheduled for October 24, 1956.

It was a sign of the good news and a good news story. The November 12, 1956, edition of *LIFE Magazine* had Rosalind Russell as Auntie Mame on the cover and Margaret Towner as the first "lady" minister in the "Close-Up" feature on page 151.[3] Rosalind Russell was in a feather boa, kicking up her heels;

Margaret Towner was in a borrowed clergy robe, kneeling. The photo essay was titled "A First Lady Minister in Robes of a New Role." The first picture was of two women pinning up the hem of a robe Margaret had borrowed for her ordination, the caption noting that Miss Towner "is only five feet, two inches tall." The robe ordered by her mother hadn't arrived in time, and the host pastor appealed to his colleagues in the area for a loaner. The Rev. Forster Freeman, remembered by Margaret as "reasonably short," offered his. But the robe was still too long, so while the invited guests enjoyed a pre-service buffet supper, two women who had come from the Allentown church took needle and thread and tailored the robe to fit. "I had worn church robes before," Margaret was quoted as saying, "but this one was the most beautiful."

Along with captions and quotes, the photographs, taken by the famous Alfred Eisenstaedt, followed the events of Margaret Towner's ordination day. One picture showed "Miss Towner" answering the ordination questions ("I concentrated hard on the questions . . . and on the answers. . . . I constantly asked God for strength and dedication."). Another captured the laying on of hands ("I felt a renewed dedication . . . I was shaking like anything."). The bulletin from that evening's service reveals that the organist played "Now Thank We All Our God," the congregation sang "Spirit of God" and "Come Labor On," the assistant pastor from the Allentown church read Acts 8:26–40 (Philip and the Ethiopian eunuch), and the senior pastor preached a sermon called "The Business of Preaching." The title and topic would seem to be an odd choice, since Margaret Towner was called as a minister of Christian education, with a clear understanding that her business would *not* be preaching. She was told in that service, "I hope you will be the shepherd of the flock and not their pet lamb."

The Rev. Margaret Towner returned to her church in Allentown and resumed her work in Christian education. She never preached in that congregation, with the exception of small gatherings of the Women's Association. She never presided at the Table, but was sent to take communion to the home bound. To those who opposed the ordination of women on the grounds "that women will move in and take over (men's) jobs" she said, "There is too much work to be done to allow any jealousy." From those who opposed an increase in her compensation on the grounds that she would eventually marry and be taken care of by a husband, she learned that there was too much work to be done to allow any equality. It was not until her next call to First Presbyterian Church in Kalamazoo, Michigan, that she had much opportunity to preach, and not until her last call at the Kettle Moraine Parish in southeastern Wisconsin that she achieved compensation equity with male colleagues. By that time, women were moving into the ministry in greater numbers—and there was still much work to be done.[4]

Margaret Towner sought me out in 1973. I was a student at Carroll College, majoring in religion with an eye toward seminary and working part-time in youth ministry at the First Presbyterian Church of Waukesha, Wisconsin. Margaret had just become one of the copastors of a yoked parish in the area and was looking for help with their high school program. We did some youth work together until I left for seminary in 1974. She was the first woman minister I had known, and she had become a model, mentor, and, as I still fondly call her, my "spiritual mother."

First Presbyterian Church in Waukesha was also the church home of Elder Lois H. Stair, the first woman to be elected to the position of Moderator of the General Assembly. I met Lois in 1971, just as I was graduating from high school. That year the commissioners from the Presbytery of Milwaukee had back-row seats at the General Assembly—meeting in Rochester, appropriately. Before the day of the convention-hall jumbotron (large screens), the youth advisory delegate from Milwaukee had to stand on her chair to see the elder who had vacated the seat next to her. The seat was assigned to Elder Commissioner Lois Stair, who had left her chair for the podium, to stand for Moderator of the 183rd General Assembly of the United Presbyterian Church U.S.A. Before the day of automated voting, commissioners cast written ballots that were counted by hand. It was a long, suspenseful evening. There were four candidates, three men, and three ballots. Lois Stair was elected on a close third ballot, 392 to 380. The convention hall erupted with joy and disbelief, and I almost fell off my chair. Acknowledging the trust that had been placed in her, she said, "Here I am, standing in the need of prayer."

I was still standing on my chair and remembered that I had been entrusted with a dime and a phone number. My job: to place a collect call back to Waukesha with whatever the news was to activate the phone tree. It was some of the best news I ever had the privilege to tell.

Lois Stair and the church stood in the need of a lot of prayer that week and the year that followed. It was a difficult assembly, and as an eighteen-year-old high school senior from Franklin, Wisconsin, thinking about the ministry, it was eye opening and formative. Racism and sexism reared their ugly heads, and there were tumultuous debates around the Vietnam War, conscientious objection, South Africa, the arms race, and reproductive rights. The recommendations from the Committee on Women were controversial. Pastor nominating committees were urged to interview at least one woman; presbyteries were directed to elect women to chair committees in equal numbers to men. Commissioners applauded and cheered when a portion of that report was voted down, and Moderator Stair responded without hesitation, "It is bitter to have defeat applauded. Please respect one another in diversity."

Lois was provided with a small office downtown, but she cleaned out her cupboards and set up an office at home, conducting moderatorial business from her kitchen table. I was living in a nearby Carroll dorm, and when she had some time on a rare home landing, we'd sit at that table and talk about her travels and travails, my interests in the ministry, and our commitments to the church.

These two remarkable women, Margaret Towner and Lois Stair, were anchors and advocates during the turbulence of my seminary years, all the while navigating their own rough waters in the church. It was during this time that Margaret chaired the General Assembly Task Force on Language about God. The first report on inclusive language was titled "Opening the Door"—an apt description of the state of that debate in the late 1970s and of the stories of Margaret's ministry and Lois's leadership.

Margaret Towner had already opened the way to my ordination, but in the fall of 1977 the hand that held open the door was laid on my head. She was a member of the presbytery commission, giving the charge to the candidate and standing before me as I knelt on the chancel steps of Heritage Presbyterian Church, where I had confirmed my baptismal faith just ten years before. I remember being enveloped by the bodies and extended hands of old friends and new colleagues; eyes closed and in a womblike warmth and darkness, I could feel my elder-parents behind me and smell my mother's perfume. A soloist sang, "Sometimes I Wish My Eyes Hadn't Been Opened," and the congregation followed with "Be Thou My Vision." Sister seminarians had come from Louisville; my mother's curious and dubious Lutheran relatives had come from a farming community nearby; students and classmates from Carroll College were there; my former Sunday school teachers and future partners in ministry had come to lay on hands in blessing and offer hands in welcome. It was Thanksgiving season; there was a cornucopia of fall flowers on my grandmother's lace tablecloth at the reception. At long last it was a day of harvested labor, the fruits of the labors of many, and great thanksgiving. The next day I preached and presided at the Table—in one of the churches in the parish served by Margaret Towner.

A month later I moved to a large, drafty upper flat in Milwaukee. I would officially become the assistant pastor at Immanuel Presbyterian Church on January 1, but eager to begin, I had asked if I could be there for the Christmas services. It was December 21, 1977, my twenty-fifth birthday. My parents arrived with a Christmas tree and brandy Manhattans. The senior pastor arrived with a coffee cake and a bulletin for Sunday's service. I'm sure I felt that, at age twenty-five, I had arrived. But, in Winston Churchill's memorable words, it was only the end of the beginning.

I was disappointed when the offer made by the Immanuel associate pastor nominating committee was to hire me as an assistant rather than call me as an associate pastor. I was young, they explained, and inexperienced. And female? If all went well they would extend a call after a year. If I "fit"? If the congregation didn't have a fit? The Women's Association gave me a robe, a black Geneva gown tailored to fit. My assignment was to rebuild the church school. The Christian education path that I had eschewed in seminary I now embraced with gusto. I loved the work, the people, and the church, and I deeply desired an opportunity to live my calling.

In nine months a call was offered, and I served as associate pastor for the next ten years. In that time both the pastor, William H. Johnstone, and I had earned Doctor of Ministry degrees from McCormick Theological Seminary. The session had done a staffing study and in 1989, while it was still constitutionally allowable, called both ministers as copastors. We took this step with encouragement from the denominational office serving women in ministry, who urged us to "name what is", that is, to claim the collegiality that had evolved, and to give gender equality to staff ministry. We served as copastors until my colleague's retirement in 1997, when, after another staffing study, I became the pastor and then head of staff. The first new associate pastor was a young woman, just graduated from seminary; the full-time associate pastor who followed her was a woman my age, just graduated from seminary. When the church considered calling a third full-time minister, questions I never dreamed would be questions emerged: Will all of our ministers be women? *Should* all of our ministers be women? Would a male minister fit?

As women in the ministry of the Word and Sacrament mark fifty years, I will mark twenty-nine years of ordained ministry at Immanuel Presbyterian Church—in five different positions! My responsibilities have changed; I have changed; the church has changed; the neighborhood has changed, . . .

And the ministry has changed.

When Margaret Towner was honorably retired by the Presbytery of Milwaukee in 1990, it was truly "the end of the beginning." She was completing a distinctive and distinguished career in active ministry that included standing for Moderator of the General Assembly the year the United Presbyterian Church U.S.A. celebrated the twenty-fifth anniversary of women in ordained ministry, and serving as Vice Moderator that year. I was asked to offer the words of commendation and thanks at her service of retirement:

> The ordination of women is not a settled issue in our own denomination or in the Christian communion. The beginning that began with Margaret Towner in 1956 is a continuing story—and a continuing struggle. The con-

stitutional affirmations of the 'fifties are the attitudinal challenges of [today]. Margaret's ministry has spanned the critical years between women as ministers being the exception and women as ministers becoming a norm. She has seen it all, heard it all—and borne it all, with humor and grace. Margaret has known that the human heart and the institutional church change slowly; she has also witnessed to the truth that the Holy Spirit works powerfully. . . .

It was a combination of circumstances by which Margaret became the first woman ordained in the Presbyterian Church. But it was Margaret's choice to be a shepherd and advocate, mentor and sister to those of us who followed. . . .

Margaret Towner has almost 1,600 daughters . . . clergywomen who have followed her through that door. . . .

When Margaret Towner was ordained, Lilian Alexander told her, "You are my daughter. Those who follow you will be your daughters." Never a "pet lamb," Margaret Towner was always a shepherd of the flock, and one of the flocks she tended was the next generation of clergywomen. We were often in her home for a gathering and a meal, joined by her mother, Dorothy, and Heidi, the St. Bernard. As she and I reminisced for this essay, I asked her what compelled her constant efforts in shepherding and "big-sistering." She replied that she saw the need for women to support one another "from the beginning, with women elders. I valued the communion of women clergy and elders. We needed to nourish that." That's when she shared Lilian Alexander's words, "Those who follow will be your daughters." And, Margaret added, "You gals have really been close to my heart."

"As God's chosen ones, holy and beloved, clothe yourselves with compassion, kindness, humility, meekness, and patience, [forbearance, forgiveness]. . . . Above all, clothe yourselves with love, which binds everything together in perfect harmony" (Col. 3:12–14). It has been an imperfect harmony, sometimes downright dissonant. The little angels sang a different song, and the pet lambs bleated. Neither the choir nor the flock would ever be the same. Against the overwhelming patriarchy of church and society, Scripture and tradition, the question many women in ministry asked one another and ourselves was, "Could we wear these robes, this ministry?" It was not a question of ability or legitimacy, but of integrity and fit. The church did not robe us with the opportunities we sought or the authority we were due. The words of theology and worship didn't match our gender. Worship wasn't styled to our voice. The ministry had been tailored to men; leadership was patterned on an unReformed and unreforming hierarchy, and although ordination could be stretched to fit women it was not sized for men and women who are gay and lesbian.

For many, women's work in the church became the process of rejecting and refuting; discovering, rediscovering, and celebrating the contributions of women, from Thekla to Julian to Elizabeth Cady Stanton and all the unnamed mothers of the faith; reappropriating and reappreciating Scripture; renaming and re-imagining God. Women in ministry have undertaken the critical and creative work of cultivating a tradition that is richer than we were taught to know, balancing the interpretation of Scripture with the weight of our witness, recalibrating worship to put God at the center and regard all persons equal— in the pew or in the pulpit or at the Table and font. In a broken and fearful church and world the Spirit has given us "courage to pray without ceasing . . . to unmask idolatries in Church and culture, to hear the voices of people long silenced, and to work with others for justice, freedom and peace."[5] It has been a sorting and a sifting, and what is slowly emerging, here and there, now and again, in discord seeking resolution and inequities seeking redress, are new harmonies, new styles, new faithfulness.

"As God's chosen ones, holy and beloved" we have put on Christ and clothed ourselves with the gifts given for ministry. "Above all," we have worn the durable and beautiful and timeless love of God. I am thankful for this story, for this struggle, for this holy calling, for the peace of Christ that consoles and compels, for the wisdom of those who have gone before, and for those who have been sisters and brothers in this ministry. I wear the borrowed robe, and it has started to feel like my own. I hear the voices of the ones who wove and stitched stories that are the very fabric of our faith. Listen! A sewer went out to sew. . . . We wear the robe that is our own. Classic, contemporary, no matter, it is part of our fiber, our blood and bone. I think of Margaret Towner, trading that borrowed robe for one given to her by her mother, and then sending that well-worn robe to a newly ordained minister in Africa, "who loved it." I think of Kathleen Norris putting on her grandmother's jacket and feeling her faith wrapped around her. I think of Tabitha making robes for the marginalized women of Joppa. I think of the marginalized woman touching Jesus' garment, healed by her faith and sent in peace and freedom. I think of Paul declaring that we have put on Christ in our baptism.

Anniversaries evoke memories and hopes. I think of all those to whom the robe of ordained ministry has been denied, in denial of the oneness of our baptismal faith. I think of those one hundred women in 1929 and hear their voices resonating in the unrest of the church today, resolute "that the church can best be served by making it possible for all members of the church to find their place of service without other discrimination than ability and capacity." I think of the unnumbered women and men of today's church and offer my own voice on behalf of those with ability and capacity who suffer the exclusion once borne by women and now suffered by persons who are gay and lesbian. I offer my own conviction and experience as an assurance to those who fear the opening of our ordination standards so that all persons may be called to all ministries of the church.

I hope that remembering the journey women made toward ordination will free the church to, in Lilian Alexander's words, "follow the spirit" of Christ "and open the doors of His ministry to all." I hope that the church will have the integrity to name what "is indeed anomalous" in our own day, the humility to stand in the need of prayer and take to heart Lois Stair's admonition to "respect one another in diversity," and the good sense to look at the church and the world and say with Margaret Towner, "There is too much work to be done to allow any fear" about who is called to ministry. I hope that my ministry will be a witness to the graceful strength of my foremothers.

Enter a new day.

Chapter 4

# "It Takes a Village"

## Cynthia M. Campbell

*Cynthia M. Campbell is the ninth president of McCormick Theological Seminary in Chicago and the Cyrus McCormick Professor of Church and Ministry. Ordained in 1974 by the Presbytery of San Gabriel, she has served over ten years in congregational ministry and seventeen years in theological education.*

*T*he African proverb "It takes a village to raise a child" is just as true of sustaining a call to ministry as it is to nurturing a human being to maturity. Many, many people have been part of my call to ministry, and without significant individuals and communities of faith along the way, I am certain that I could not have sustained a life of ministry and commitment to leadership in the church. What has been true for me is also true for others. Being part of those "villages" of support and encouragement is required of all of us who care about the future and vitality of the church.

From the time I was twelve or thirteen, I knew what I wanted to be when I grew up, but I never told anyone. Actually, I knew *who* I wanted to be. I wanted to be the Rev. Dr. H. Ganse Little, pastor of the Pasadena Presbyterian Church, the church in which I was raised. He was an immensely gifted preacher—widely read, given to an expository style of preaching, courageous in addressing issues in the late 1950s and early 1960s, such as fair housing, sexual ethics and the cold war. He was an ecumenical leader both in Southern California and nationally. His election as Moderator of the General Assembly of the UPCUSA in 1966 was part of a strategy to win approval of the Confession of 1967.

I became a student of his sermons. Every Saturday, the text and title of Sunday's sermon were printed in the newspaper. Each week, I underlined and dated the text in my Bible (actually, an interesting record of the work of a nonlectionary preacher). As the years went by, I became reasonably proficient at guessing how Dr. Little would approach the text and what direction the sermon would take. Years later when I was invited to preach at PPC, members of the congregation said, "Your preaching reminds us so much of Dr. Little." Scarcely surprising, since he was my first teacher, although he had no idea I was his student!

What drew me to the church and to ministry as a young adult is in fact what continues to sustain my life today. For me as a young person, the church was a community of people (both adults and peers) who accepted me for who I was, a community where my gifts for service and leadership were welcomed and encouraged, and a community of worship that prized both beauty (especially in music) and intellectual rigor. I cannot imagine my life without weekly participation in a worshiping community, and I cannot imagine life without work in which I am challenged to articulate Christian faith in the face of the demands of a changed and ever-changing world.

It was years before I admitted my ambition to anyone, myself included. At Occidental College, I found my intellectual home in philosophy but was frustrated by a department that was reluctant to entertain religious or theological questions. I went on to seminary almost by accident. On recommendation of the campus chaplain, I applied for a fellowship that would provide for one year of theological education at any seminary or divinity school in the country. Harvard Divinity School confirmed the intellectual part of my call: namely, to love God with all my mind.

It took a year-long internship to confirm the call of my heart to parish ministry. I spent the year between my second and third years in seminary with the pastor and people of Grace Presbyterian Church in Little Rock, Arkansas. I was their sixth full-time intern, and they were deeply committed to being a "teaching church." While there was a basic job description, interns were encouraged to shape their work based on their own talents and interests. Without this challenging year, I would never have been able to say with assurance that I wanted to be a pastor. Nor would I have had the confidence later on to continue to pursue a call to parish ministry positions when doors were continually closed to me.

It is clear to me that I would not be in ministry were it not for the outstanding examples of ministry I experienced growing up. In addition to Ganse Little, I was blessed to know ministers and directors of Christian education, church musicians, professors of Bible and philosophy, presbytery and synod staff, and dedicated church school teachers. All of these women and men evidenced the qualities I have come to admire most: enthusiasm for the church, intellectual curiosity, courage when facing difficult issues, and deep commitment to Jesus Christ.

While it goes without saying that there were almost no women "role models" for the positions I have held (either in the church or in theological education), there have always been mentors, colleagues, and friends—men and women—who have encouraged me along the way. I was ordained in 1974 by the Presbytery of San Gabriel (only the second woman candidate in their history) after what I recall as a long and fairly grueling oral examination. After a couple of fairly routine questions from the committee, the floor was opened to the presbytery as a whole. A member of the faculty at Occidental College who had the reputation of being a rigorous examiner (but who was also a dear friend of mine), asked me to explain to the body why they should vote to ordain me when Paul seemed to be quite clear that "women should be silent in the churches. For they are not permitted to speak, but should be subordinate, as the law also says" (1 Cor. 14:34). My friend knew that I had made careful study of this and other related passages with Krister Stendahl, whose critical exegetical work had prepared the way for the ordination of women in several of the Lutheran churches in Europe. My answer took almost twenty minutes, after which the presbytery was more than ready to suspend the examination!

The day of my ordination, June 30, 1974, is as vivid a memory as any I have. I invited Ganse Little back to Pasadena to preach the sermon. He chose John 21:9–10 as his text: "When they had gone ashore, they saw a charcoal fire there, with fish on it, and bread. Jesus said to them, 'Bring some of the fish that you have just caught.'" His point was this: after gathering in the net full of fish, the disciples come ashore to meet the risen Christ. A fire is already there. Bread and fish are cooking, but Jesus invites them to bring what they have. It is just so, he said, with ministry. God *could* do all that would be needed without us, but God *chooses* to do otherwise. God invites us to bring who we are, *whoever we are*, and what we have to be used for God's mission. The empowering implication was not lost on me then, and I have preached this sermon a dozen times at ordination and installation services.

Like many women who entered the ministry in the 1970s, I have had many experiences of being "the first" or "the only" woman to serve in various capacities. My first call was as assistant pastor (later associate) of the Northminster United Presbyterian Church in Dallas, where in the fall of 1974 (according to the *Dallas Morning News*) I was the only woman in *any denomination* serving in congregational ministry. Because I remained in Dallas to do doctoral work at Southern Methodist University, I did a great deal of supply preaching in what is now Grace Presbytery. I stopped counting after two dozen the number of churches where I was the first woman ever to preach. When I was called to serve as pastor of the First Presbyterian Church of Salina, Kansas (first or second congregation of over one thousand members to call a woman as pastor/head of staff), *USA Today* carried the announcement as their "factoid" for the state of Kansas the day after the congregation voted. There was less

Cynthia M. Campbell speaks at her inauguration as president of McCormick Theological Seminary in 1995. (*Courtesy of McCormick Theological Seminary.*)

publicity when I was the first woman named to serve as president of one of our degree-granting Presbyterian seminaries, perhaps because education is a more familiar role for women. Even today, however, women lead only about ten percent of theological schools in the United States and Canada.

What can be said about the leadership of women in the Presbyterian Church seventy-five years after women were first ordained as elders and nearly fifty years after women were ordained to the ministry of Word and Sacrament? The percentage of women who are preparing for ministry has increased steadily, but the number of ordained women who leave (especially parish) ministry is also high. The number of women holding denominational executive positions and teaching in our seminaries has increased significantly. While the number of women serving as pastors of churches with over one thousand members has increased, resistance to the leadership of women as "senior pastors/head of staff" continues. Not long ago, I received a call requesting names for a large Presbyterian congregation. When all three suggestions I made were women, the committee member said, "I guess we are ready to *consider* the idea of calling a woman as pastor."

The question about the leadership of women in the future is one that can be asked and answered only in the context of the future of the Presbyterian Church as a whole. It is true that our denomination has declined both in real numbers and in percentage of the American population. But that fact taken by itself ignores the fact that there are thousands of active, vibrant, and vital Presbyterian congregations in rural areas, suburbs, and downtown neighborhoods all across America. It is time for us to stop worrying about numbers and concentrate on sustaining and developing new healthy congregations. And *the* critical factor for the health of congregations is outstanding pastoral leadership.

If we as Presbyterians want to continue a lively Christian presence, a way of living the Christian life marked by the engagement of our faith in God with the real needs of the world, we must call, prepare, and support leaders who embody the kind of church life we want to sustain. I followed a call to ministry because of what I saw in the lives of those who raised me in the faith. The same thing is needed today. We who lead the church (as pastors, educators, elders, deacons, teachers, and members) need to be aware of our capacity for inspiring and mentoring young people to consider ministry and service.

In presenting the possibility of call to ministry, it is important that we remember how we in the Reformed tradition think about these matters. A hallmark of the Reformation was the renewed emphasis on the place and role of the whole people of God. Texts such as 1 Peter 2:9 served as the inspiration for this shift: "But you are a chosen race, a royal priesthood, a holy nation, God's own people, in order that you might proclaim the mighty acts of him who called you out of darkness into his marvelous light." From this perspective, ministry is first of all the responsibility of the "people of God" as a whole and only secondarily the task of those persons set aside for or called to "ministry." As the Body of Christ, the church is charged to continue Christ's "ministry of reconciliation" (as Paul calls it) in and for the world. Happily, this perspective has been recovered by the church as a whole, as evidenced by the documents of Vatican II and by the ecumenical consensus document produced by the World Council of Churches: *Baptism, Eucharist and Ministry.*

According to this view, ministry is what all believers are commissioned to do by virtue of baptism. When we think about ordained ministries in the life of the church, we must first remember baptism, the sacrament that unites us individually and collectively to Jesus Christ. By means of the water of baptism we are not only made clean from sin and promised new life; we are incorporated into Christ's body and thereby become responsible for continuing his ministry in the world. Each believer individually and the entire church collectively is called to ministry in response to God's grace in Jesus Christ.

I feel fortunate to have been raised in a family where this idea of "calling" or vocation was part of our self-understanding. When I was growing up, both of my parents worked full-time. My father was an accountant, and my mother was a medical technologist. Each of them ended up in their professions as a means to support themselves and their families in the postdepression years. In neither case was the work they did their first choice, but in both cases they recognized that they had suitable skills and that their work was of service to others. Over the years, I came to understand that God gives gifts and abilities to each person and that these are best used when they serve some common or larger good. In this way, one fulfills humanity's "chief end," to glorify God.

Our family had dinner together virtually every night. Table conversation consisted mainly in sharing what each of us had done that day. By the time I was in school, it was clear that my "job" (for the time being at least) was being a student. I was expected to share my activities and accomplishments and challenges with my parents just as they shared theirs with each other and with me. The vocation of our "everyday" work was seen as part of our larger commitment as individuals and as a family to live in response to God's good gifts to us.

The call to ministry and specifically to ordination must be discussed within this context. Within that ministry, some are called to particular service as ministers of Word and Sacrament, elders, and deacons. It is critically important to remember that, for Presbyterians, "ordained ministry" refers to all three offices and that the process of "call" should be stressed for each of them. As a pastor, I have often found it difficult to interpret this idea of call during the nominating and electing process. The idea of being "called" to the ministry of elder or deacon is challenging for some who see this as just another job as a volunteer or as one more civic duty to be fulfilled. This view represents the failure of the community (as well as the individual) to understand the offices of elder and deacon as means by which God shapes, guides, and cares for the church. At the other end of the spectrum, I have encountered those who take these offices so seriously that they say they feel unworthy even to consider serving. This represents a failure to understand that, in a certain way, all of us are "unworthy" and able to serve only by the grace of God that works in and through us.

Lifting up the call to ministry of Word and Sacrament is just as challenging. For the past several years, various denominational offices, the Presbyterian seminaries, and local congregations have undertaken projects to identify young adults with gifts for ministry. Much of this activity has been funded by the Lilly Endowment, which is committed to improving the quality of pastoral leadership in American religious life. Significant gains have been made: more students are coming to seminary shortly after completing their undergraduate studies. Many have been "recruited" to ministry through the Presbyterian Young Adult Volunteer Program. Other programs have been designed to help new (and especially younger) seminary graduates enter ministry and succeed in their first call.

It seems to me, however, that entering the ministry of Word and Sacrament today (for both men and women) is more difficult than I remember it being thirty years ago. As local churches experience the stress of recent economic downturns and membership loss, they become more demanding of ministers to come in and provide ready solutions to their problems. As presbyteries become the venue in which denominational battles are fought, the newly ordained find themselves caught in the cross fire rather than welcomed into a fellowship of pastors.

When I entered the ministry, the congregations I served as an intern and as a "first call" both understood that I was still learning to be a minister, *and* they understood that it was their job to help me learn and grow. Likewise, various pastors, educators, and lay leaders in presbyteries took it upon themselves to welcome me and mentor me into the church beyond the congregation. I will never forget being with leaders of Presbyterian Women at a time when I was very discouraged about remaining in parish ministry. I was with them at a conference center to do a series of Bible studies on women in leadership. The presentations went well, and I felt deeply affirmed by their response. In a late-night conversation with a small group, I shared some of the pain, frustration, and doubt I was experiencing. In the strongest possible terms, they affirmed my gifts and told me how important my continuing in ministry was as a sign of hope for them. Their love and encouragement helped me see beyond the challenges I then faced, and their support helped me continue to hear God's call.

If the church is to benefit from the leadership abilities that God has clearly given to women, it must be willing to support and encourage them in fulfilling their ministries. Most women entering ministry today expect to be able to be pastors and raise their children. This may require adjustments of workload, office hours, and other important accommodations. Nominating committees need to take into account gaps in employment taken to fulfill commitments to family. Presbyteries will need to find more creative ways to use the professional skills and energy of women (and men) who are seeking part-time rather than full-time ministry while raising young children. Congregations should consider assisting the minister's spouse (both men and women) find adequate employment in the community in order to make relocation possible.

Finally, the future of women in ministry cannot be discussed apart from the theological issue of language about God. Regardless of the fact that the Presbyterian understanding of ministry and ordination does *not* see the pastor (or elder) as "representing" God, the general cultural understanding of religious leadership does make that connection. As long as the way we talk about God is limited to male titles and masculine pronouns, women as religious leaders will always seem just a bit "off" or not the norm. Theologically, we *know* that God is neither male nor female and, as a theologian friend of mine puts it, the One who created gender is not bound by it. But when we rely only on one type of language, metaphor, and symbol, we deny in practice what we know to be true. In the Brief Statement of Faith, we declare that God is beyond the confines of human gender when we say, "Like a mother who will not forsake her nursing child, like a father who runs to welcome the prodigal home, God is faithful still." This is followed by the bold affirmation that God "calls women and men to all offices of the church." This puts us as Presbyterians out of step with some of the largest and fastest-growing Christian movements in the U.S. (the Southern Baptist Church, the Roman Catholic Church, and the mega-church movement), which either explicitly or implicitly deny women significant leadership positions. But Presbyterians have never argued that the validity of a theological view could be determined solely by the number of people agreeing to it.

I am deeply grateful for all the opportunities I have had to serve God through the ministry of Word and Sacrament in the Presbyterian Church (U.S.A.), and I want to continue to encourage and support the women and men that God will continue to call. No one person explicitly "called" me to ministry, but the words and actions of many women and men over the years brought me to discern a call and have sustained me through the years. Those of us who have received such gifts are even more responsible than others to be part of God's voice of extending the call to others and offering our support, encouragement, and care to those who come to take their places in leadership and service. Just as ministry is the work of "the whole people of God," so it is the community as a whole that is responsible for raising up leaders for the future.

# Chapter 5

# Didn't Know Where I Was Headed

## Marj Carpenter

*Marj Carpenter, a lifelong Presbyterian, served as an ordained dea-con before being ordained as an elder. She was a journalist in Texas for many years before becoming the director of the news service of the Presbyterian Church U.S. and later the Presbyterian Church (U.S.A.). Marj served as Moderator of the General Assembly and promoted "mission, mission, mission!"*

*H*ow did we get there? I never remember a Sunday that I wasn't in a Presbyterian church somewhere, unless I was in a place that had no Presbyterian church. One of my earliest memories is sitting in the church pew with my grandmother and my brother while Dad and Mom sang in the choir. My grandpa was angry at the church and was at home. This makes us kind of a typical Presbyterian family.

Later, when I was in the youth group in Mercedes, Texas, I wasn't satisfied unless I persuaded kids from other churches who weren't attending youth groups to come to ours. Some of them, in their adulthood, have ended up as Presbyterian members and elders.

During my teenage years, a large part of our youth group went to Westminster Encampment on the Shreiner campus at Kerrville. The Rev. Charles Tucker took us in an old homemade trailer. We waited tables to help pay our registration. A lot of the leadership of the Presbyterian Church, even nationally, came out of those camp sessions. I remember sitting on the hillside at sundown singing, "Now the Day Is Over" and how special it was.

Later, when I attended college at Texas A & I in Kingsville, I was not one of the college kids who quit going to church when away from home. My grandmother and my parents had instilled the love of the church in me. I walked sixteen blocks from the dorm to Sunday school and church, and I became president of the college youth group. I was also president of the band and the press club. I guess I just like being president.

World War II ended just as I had one more year of college. I married a returning soldier right out of college, and we moved to Odem, Texas, where there was no Presbyterian church. We drove seven miles to Sinton on Sunday, attended church, ate lunch, and came home. We both taught school in Odem.

Next, we moved to Pecos, Texas, where there was a Presbyterian church. My one-year-old daughter and I went the first Sunday we were in town. My husband did not go. There was a lot of discussion about that at home. By the third Sunday, I was in charge of the nursery Sunday school class, which I then taught for fifteen years. It was a great success. Mothers from other churches brought their children aged four and under because I taught Bible stories and children's songs. My mother and grandmother had taught me that was the way to teach Sunday school.

In that congregation, I raised my three children, saw them baptized, and saw them profess their faith. Every now and then, my husband would go to church, but we didn't count on it. At least he seemed glad that we went.

I put a lot of energy into that congregation. I taught the nursery class. I led the high school fellowship. I taught three graded children's choirs and directed the adult choir. I put on an elaborate Joy Gift program at Christmas. I was president of the Presbyterian Women after holding every other office and was on the Andrew's Committee to visit shut-in and prospective members. I also directed Bible school and Easter egg hunts. And I was always the one asked to raise funds—for choir robes, for a new baptismal font, for the candelabras, and for the lowering of the front concrete steps so the elderly could get in the church.

I also worked on the local newspaper covering wrecks, fires, murders, politics, and sports. I was the second woman sports writer in Texas. I never thought about women having difficulty in doing anything. I always just did it. There was no time that I remember worrying about being an ordained pastor or elder. It never even occurred to me that I might someday be eligible.

When my husband died at the early age of forty-four, it was my church family that supported me and my children. At that time in Pecos, we were embroiled in the national Billie Sol Estes scandal. The newspaper I worked for was right in the middle of it. Even the church was affected by all of the bitterness and anger that was going on at that time.

Certainly no women in our congregation even gave a thought to ordination, although it was the 1960s, years that the church was opening up for women. The Rev. Jack Ware had all he could do to keep members of that congregation speaking to each other. It wasn't a good time to suggest ordaining a woman officer.

About then, our newspaper was purchased and shut down, and I moved to Andrews to work on the paper there. I attended the Presbyterian church, but I also got involved in a teenage recreation center because there was nowhere for teenagers to go in that town. My girls were going off to college, and I was raising my son at home. Again, I didn't have any time to even think about being an officer in the church. My next move was to Big Spring, where I worked on the newspaper there. Suddenly, I became very active in the church again.

A teenager named Hugh Porter asked me after church, "Will you teach our Sunday school class? Nobody wants us." That week I began what became a very successful youth group that grew from three to seventy-two in a three-year period. We had a new pastor, the Rev. Bill Henning, and he helped me get the youth group going. He had worked for the national office of the Presbyterian Church U.S. in Atlanta, and he began to make me aware of the larger church.

For the first time I was in a congregation that was encouraging women to serve in office. This preacher persuaded six of us to venture forth. Three (including me) became deacons, and three became elders. We were feeling very humble about this new development. There really weren't too many ordained women yet serving in all of Tres Rios Presbytery. There was one saint in our congregation who helped to keep it that way. Such saints were probably in other congregations, too. In our church, this lady helped more people than anyone in the congregation, but she refused to put money in an offering plate passed by a woman and refused to take communion from a woman.

Well, there we were. The women deacons helped greet. We helped lock up. We helped keep the property in order, but we didn't usher or take up the offering or serve communion.

Suddenly, there was a special youth Sunday. They asked me to send four youths to usher and take up the offering. Three boys volunteered. Then, one girl volunteered. I said, "Go for it." I deliberately put her on the side where the saint sat. When she handed the saint the offering plate, Lois Ivey smiled. The saint hesitated, then put in her offering envelope, and it was all over. From then on, women could take up the offering and serve communion in that congregation.

I was the elected chair of the board of deacons. The following year I was ordained as an elder. Anyone that has been ordained as an elder knows how impressive it is to receive the laying on of hands. It takes you back in history and is very meaningful. I was later installed as elder in other churches, and it was always meaningful. I was in elder training under Bill Henning, Ray Riddle, Al Winn, and Flynn V. Long—some of the very best in the denomination. It never had occurred to me to think about the meaning of an elder's vows until I was one myself. After that, every time I took part in an ordination of elders, I always had a very sober moment of peace and said a silent prayer. I was praying that there would always be Presbyterians who take very seriously the office and the responsibility of being an elder.

I later served in Big Spring as clerk of the session, and it was along about then that I was asked to go to Atlanta to apply for news and information director of the Presbyterian Church U.S. My work with the national church led me in two different directions. I dealt with secular religion writers all over the country. I tried to assist them with information for their news columns, and I often found myself trying to explain the intricacies of the Presbyterian denomination. The other direction I went was getting out into the world to see what Presbyterians were doing in the mission field. It was in that capacity that I learned what elder meant in other parts of the world.

One of the first places I went was South Korea. I had a bus schedule in my hand and Korean cash in my purse. I also had the assurance that missionaries would meet me at each scheduled stop. At each stop I met Korean Presbyterians. I found out rather quickly what a high regard they place on the office of elder. They addressed me as Elder Carpenter and invariably expressed surprise that I was a female.

That was in 1981, and fourteen years later, in 1995, I made a fourth trip to South Korea. It was the year that one of the two major Presbyterian denominations in the country had voted to ordain women. What a celebration we had at the Presbyterian Women's building! I posed for a photo out in the patio with over one hundred beautiful Korean women in their colorful dresses. I had on a dark red suit and looked like a thorn among the roses.

In a country where there are now some nine million Presbyterians, it was wonderful to celebrate this accomplishment with the women. The following spring, they sent me a ticket to return so that the Presbyterian Women's University in Seoul could present me with an honorary doctorate. They presented it with these words: "Thank you for working for the dignity of all people."

Two other honorary doctorates have been presented to me, by Austin College in Sherman, Texas, and Presbyterian College in Clinton, South Carolina. Each time the office of elder was emphasized, as it was when I spoke at other institutions' graduations, including San Francisco Presbyterian Seminary, Alma College, and Shreiner University, back where I went to youth gatherings in my teenage years. I've spoken at many of our other colleges and universities, and I've spoken at all of our seminaries. Invariably, it is mentioned that I'm an elder.

If I hadn't been ordained an elder, I would not have been eligible to be nominated by Tres Rios Presbytery for the office of Moderator of the General Assembly in 1995. That was a tough decision for me because I thought my newspaper days had given me too many rough edges for that highly respected office. It was encouragement from friends and a lot of praying that got me through. My three children were very supportive, but I had a feeling they really thought I was out of my mind.

Moderator Marj Carpenter addresses the 1995 General Assembly in Cincinnati, Ohio. (*Courtesy of the author.*)

When the moment arrived for the actual vote, and the advisory votes were taken, I led in every category, which made me feel both humble and hopeful. I went on to win on the first ballot. Later, my son asked me, "Why was the ecumenical [overseas partner churches] vote the lowest percentage? You know people all over the world." I answered, "You have to understand that it was not against me personally. In many of those countries, women cannot be ordained."

It made me recall that when I had visited a General Assembly in Guatemala, there were no women allowed in the hall, except one woman missionary, one woman editor, and me. The women were under the tents in the kitchen area cooking the noon meal. I was invited to speak briefly. I commended them for their excellent assembly but reminded them that the first people that Jesus spoke to on his resurrection were women. I concluded with "I think I'll go out to the kitchen and talk to the women, as well." Needless to say, that was not the most popular speech I ever made in the world—except in the kitchen.

Although I am not an ordained minister, I have preached in over six thousand of our churches. This is because Presbyterians are hungry to hear about mission, and they want to hear from somebody who has seen it. The first time I spoke in the pulpit I was terrified. I was working at the PCUS headquarters in Atlanta when a small congregation in a church on the Alabama border called and asked if I would come to tell them about a trip several of us made to Africa in 1983.

I had been making talks at country churches in the area at church suppers and at Sunday school. So I thought that's what I was getting into in this case, but when I got there, early enough for Sunday school, I was told that I was preacher of the day. I was also told that the congregation really didn't like women preachers, but they wanted to hear about Africa. I desperately planned the Great Commission as my Scripture and tried my best to "wax eloquently." It went well, much to my surprise. Later in the week, I received a letter from the session thanking me. They said, "Even the people who hate women preachers enjoyed your sermon."

That same year I was invited to Little Rock to speak at presbytery—again on Africa. I took a tray of slides to show, but we met in a sanctuary with clear glass windows and no shades, so you couldn't show slides. The presbyter said, "Oh, just run off at the mouth. You'll do alright." I did, and it worked.

From then on, I seemed to have gotten on a preaching treadmill. It's been twenty-two years, and I've never run out of invitations. In the process, of course, I have seen an awful lot of the Presbyterian Church, and I have never ceased to be amazed at how wonderful it is to be Presbyterian. I feel honored to be an elder.

Two of my heroines along the way are both former women moderators. One is Sara B. Moseley, who was the first female moderator of the Presbyterian Church U.S. in 1974. This was two years before I was an elder. The other is Harriet Nelson, who was the first female moderator after reunion. Going through several African countries with her, her husband, John, and several others, is a memory I will always cherish.

Interestingly enough, women were the hardest on ordained women. Right after reunion, all of the different women's groups met together on a retreat in Ohio. It included Presbyterian Women, Racial Ethnic Women, Clergy Women, and the Committee on Advocacy for Women. You would have thought they all hated each other. The old song about knowing Christians by their love was obviously not on the agenda. Isabel Rodgers, also later a moderator of the General Assembly, was leading the Bible study. I was reporting on the meeting for the church news briefs. They ran out of rooms, so Izzie and I slept on cots in the basement next to an air conditioning unit that wheezed all night long. We later laughed when the two of us ended up as moderators. We got out of that basement.

All of the women moderators were particularly strong. Women like Freda Gardner, Pat Brown, Thelma Adair, the late Dorothy Bernard, and the late

Lois Stair. Lois may have been the strongest one of us all, as she wrote some ten thousand personal notes during the Angela Davis controversy and possibly saved the church.

The office of elder is highly respected all over the church, and it is viewed in a diverse manner in different parts of the world. One of the most unusual incidents involving an elder that I ever ran across occurred in Ghana. A group of us were participating in an outside worship service there. Kenneth Rogers from Virginia was preaching. The choir was decked out in discarded caps and gowns from Davidson College. Yes, they wore the caps—tassels and all. Right in the middle of the sermon, a member of the congregation ran up to the preacher, held up his hands and said, "Stop! The chief is coming, and he is the elder." We could hear the drums coming down the road. One of the group carried a rattan chair that he brought to the front. Everybody moved back and made room. The chief sat down, and a little boy began to fan him with a large fan. The drummers sat all around him. Then, the man who had stopped the sermon came forward and said, "Go." Kenneth had a puzzled moment trying to remember where he had left off. Little did he know, he was preaching to the entire session because that chief did not allow there to be but one elder, and it was him. Obviously, they didn't fully understand the Presbyterian system.

Another interesting part of being an elder in an African country is something I witnessed in Zaire (now Congo). We attended a service in a Presbyterian church there with about five thousand in attendance. As is the custom in many churches in Africa, the congregation walked up to the altar to bring gifts of chickens, corn, or other items. Some brought money that was dropped into an open strongbox. After church, the entire session went out under the shade tree and counted the money together, carefully watching each other. The money was then locked in the box and carried away by the treasurer to some unknown location. Those elders were obviously guardians of the resources. I don't know who ate the corn and chicken.

The saddest group of elders I ever saw in the world was in Serbia. The congregation there was being persecuted, and elders were dying in strange accidents on the streets. The Reformed church members were trying to slip them out of the country. Every few weeks they would stage a mock funeral and take an elder out to Hungary in a coffin with air holes and a funeral procession. The Rev. Bob Bohl, former moderator, was preaching there, and the remaining elders sat up front off to one side, kind of like a choir. They had the saddest expressions of any elders I have ever seen. No wonder.

The long and proud history of eldership in the Presbyterian Church is being carried on well by women. It has been recorded that many early Scots would die to protect the office of elder. It has also been reported that when Woodrow

Wilson was asked what the biggest honor in his life was, he did not answer that it was when he became president of the United States. He said it was when he was ordained as an elder in the Presbyterian Church.

The office of elder is noticeably absent in the growing and emerging Protestant church in the communist countries of China and North Korea. No denomination is allowed to dominate, and that leaves some confusion for the earlier Christians. I did notice that in both those countries, it is the women members who seem to be carrying on with the duties that in our churches are handled by the session. Since the office of elder is so important in South Korea, it will be interesting to see what happens if North and South Korea ever get to reunite.

There are some very tiny churches in this country that have only one or two elders. There is the story of a person assigned to reorganize small churches by working with the session. In a very small church with one elder, the organizer was told, "I'm the only one, and I don't want to be reorganized."

Once I was a guest speaker at a presbytery where a group of women attacked a small congregation that had no women elders. The discussion became heated until it was learned that the upset women were on a session that had no men elders. Their defense was, "We don't have any men who want to be elders." The other church answered, "And we have no women who want to be elders." Finally, there was a compromise, and one group agreed to try to get male members while the other agreed to try to find females. It was really an interesting confrontation.

Another interesting thing about the office of elder is how it is looked upon by other denominations. One misconception is that they are all older—which once upon a time, they were.

The biggest problem in the twenty-some-year discussions in the Consultation on Church Union was the misunderstanding in the discussion of the offices of bishop and elder. They didn't merge well, and the group began to discuss cooperative moves rather than absolute union. There are other denominations that use the term of elder.

I had one humorous incident occur to me in regard to the Latter Day Saints. I had been to the 100th anniversary of a small Presbyterian church in Idaho, just across the Utah border. They took me back to the Salt Lake City airport to fly home. When I got to the gate, all the seats were filled. There was a huge crowd. This was in the days when everybody could go to the gate. One woman with several children graciously put one on her lap and offered me a seat. I asked what the occasion was, and she told me they were seeing off two young elders who were going to Mexico. I commended her, and then made the mistake of saying, "I'm an elder." "You can't be; women can't be," I was told. I answered, "But, I'm Presbyterian, and in our church, you can be, and I'm an elder." You would have thought I had said, "I have smallpox." She gathered up her children and moved to a gate across the way and en route told all of her friends about me. It created such a stir that the Delta flight attendant told me she would upgrade me to first class if I would agree to go ahead and get on the plane early. So I did.

I'm glad we began to ordain women although there was a time that I couldn't have cared less. I know that my understanding of ordination has grown greatly through the years. When I think about who was influential along the way, I think first of my mother and grandmother. They were both strong women who worked hard for the church. I also think about preachers along the way—Charles Tucker, Ben Gillespie, Jack Ware, Bill Henning, Al Winn, Joe Harvard, Steve Lytch, and Flynn V. Long. I started to try to name national staff members and elected committee members that had helped me grow, but there were too many. I couldn't name them all, but I couldn't have made it without them—both women and men.

The wonderful thing about the Presbyterian Church is that we are like one big family. We even quarrel like family, but we also support and love each other like family. We have come a long way together. I remember one woman saying rather bitterly, "We used to only be able to teach Sunday school, sing in the choir, do the women's work, and help in the kitchen." She continued, "Now, we can be deacons, elders, and preachers, and we still get to teach Sunday school, sing in the choir, do the women's work, and help in the kitchen. I'm trying to decide if that is progress."

The answer is, "Yes, it is." Since we have gotten past those first years, some of the men pitch in and help with all of it now. We need to remember why we are doing it. We are serving our Lord Jesus Christ and helping keep our particular part of His Church alive and well in the world. My hopes are high for the future of women in the Presbyterian Church. However, these hopes will be realized only if we can move forward without cutting down the men. For a while right after women's ordination opened up, the men seemed to drop back and more or less say, "If you want to run it, run it." This was not good. The church needs the strong leadership of both working together. Gradually, the ability to share and respect each other seems to be emerging in most congregations.

All of the early ordained women seemed to be talented and strong. It has been long enough that now there are both strong and weak ordained women—both talented and less talented. There is variety, just like with the men. All of us who love the Lord and love the church can help build its future if we work together. We need to worry less about things over which we disagree and worry more about strengthening the church in the world. May it be so.

Chapter 6

# From the Kitchen to the Pulpit:
# A Korean Woman Pastor's Journey

## Choi, Moon Young

*Choi, Moon Young was born and raised in South Korea; she moved to the United States in 1987. She is associate pastor in Contra Costa Korean Presbyterian Church in California and a Ph.D. student at Graduate Theological Union in Berkeley, CA. She is the mother of Jeanne Lee and wife of Rev. Dr. Dae Sung Lee.*

*M*om, you cannot be a pastor!"
"What . . . Why?"
"Because you are a woman!"
"Then, what about your dad?"
"He can be a pastor!"
"How come?"
"Because he is a man!"

It sounds like a statement prohibiting woman's ordination that has been heard repeatedly in Christian history. It was, however, a conversation between my daughter and me when she was only two years and nine months old. My husband and I were preparing for my ordination/installation service when my daughter suddenly jumped into our conversation and made this bombshell declaration. She had seen only male pastors in her life and could not envision her mother as a pastor. I was surprised to find that this little girl already had fixed ideas of gender roles in the ecclesial vocation. My husband and I laughed aloud, and I eagerly educated my daughter that women could also become pastors.

I heard a similar response from my mother, whose Presbyterian denomination in Korea does not yet ordain women. When I disclosed my intention to be an ordained pastor, my sixty-five-year-old faithful mother responded with worries and concerns: "Can't you believe in God just as you are? You can follow Jesus as Christian educator and pastor's wife like you are right

49

now. Somehow, I find myself feeling unfamiliar and uncomfortable with a woman pastor."

Regardless of generation, I thought, the idea of a woman pastor appears new and strange in the Korean church context. These incidents are emblematic of my long struggle to be an ordained pastor.

## From the Kitchen to the Pulpit

In the fall of 1987, I arrived at Princeton Theological Seminary with anticipation of new life in the United States. While I supported my husband's study there, I felt lonely, anxious, and homesick in a new environment without close family members and friends. Even though my major was English literature and linguistics in a prestigious university in Korea, I felt insecure about my English ability. Just a few months earlier I had been a professional editor and journalist, but here I was just a housewife. There were very few Koreans in Princeton to share my difficulties. In a small student apartment, I prayed to God with tears while reading the book of Job in the Bible to find the meaning of human suffering. As I recovered from culture shock and loneliness, I began to hope that I would become a person stretching out my hands to hold the hands of someone else in need and pain. Who knew this difficult experience in Princeton was the beginning of a calling!

Moving to California was a turning point in my life. When my husband began his doctoral program at Graduate Theological Union, I enrolled in San Francisco Theological Seminary. Previously I thought my call to serve God was in the role of a pastor's wife. Now I felt God calling me to ministry.

In the first chapel service in seminary we happened to sing the hymn "Here I Am, Lord." When I sang the verses, I could not stop shedding tears with deep gratitude and heartfelt thanks.

> Here I am, Lord. Is it I, Lord? I have heard You calling in the night.
> I will go, Lord, if You lead me. I will hold Your people in my heart.[1]

Although it was certainly a challenge to start a M.Div. degree seven years after graduation from college, I was fascinated with the new life in the seminary. However, the field education requirement posed a challenge in my family relationship. Before I entered the seminary, I helped my husband's ministry, as was expected of the wives of Korean pastors. In most Korean churches, after the worship services Korean foods are served. Sharing food in ethnic churches is sharing cultural identity and nostalgia for the homeland. Pastors' wives usually play an important role in these meals.

My internship was in a different Korean church from the one my husband served. That posed a problem for both congregations and for me. When I arrived in the church for my internship, some people thought I was single. Finding that I was a married woman, especially a pastor's wife, they assumed we had some marriage problems. My husband's congregation seemed to perceive him to be a deficient pastor because his wife was not helping him.

As for myself, I felt a deep sense of guilt for going on my own journey. At times I tried to assuage my guilt by cooking and providing food for my husband's ministry in addition to working in my own church. Like many women in Korean churches, I had internalized the belief that only men, not women, were entitled to enter the pulpit. Thus I often felt inadequate and had difficulty owning my right to preach. After preaching, I would quickly rush to the kitchen as if that was where I belonged. It took a long time to develop self-confidence in the pulpit, free from this "kitchen-attachment syndrome."

## Inheriting My Grandmothers' Garden of Faith

Looking back on my childhood, I think this kitchen-attachment syndrome is also closely related to my home church experiences in Korea. I was born and raised in a Christian family and Presbyterian church in Seoul, South Korea. It is no exaggeration to say that the Protestant church in Korea started with the arrival of an American Presbyterian missionary. On Easter Sunday morning in 1885, Rev. H. G. Underwood, dispatched by the Presbyterian Church in the U.S.A., arrived as the first missionary in Korea, along with a Methodist missionary. Since then, Christianity has played an important role in the modernization of Korean society as well as in spiritual spheres. It has grown dramatically in numbers since the 1970s, and about twenty-five percent of the population in South Korea is Christian. There are many new world records in Korean churches. The biggest church and the biggest Presbyterian seminary in the world are in South Korea. Furthermore, Korea is the second largest country besides the United States to dispatch many missionaries to the world. Although there are some negative side effects due to the rapid growth, the churches in the world pay attention to the Korean church.

I have grown up with pride that I am a fourth-generation Christian, which is rare due to the relatively short history of Christianity in Korea. My paternal great-grandmother was first converted to Christianity, and her Christian faith was passed to my grandmother and my mother. I never met my great-grandmother because she died before I was born. But I remember how my grandmother was faithful and loved the words of God. My grandmother, born in 1900, like many women in her times, did not have public education and was illiterate. Yet because of her strong faith, my grandmother learned to read the Bible. In her later years, she had a stroke. I still remember how my grandmother made a great effort to copy the Bible on a faded notebook with her paralyzed left hand. Leaving her hometown, Pyeongyang, in North Korea during the Korean War, she died without returning to the homeland of her faith.[2] My mother, a college graduate and a former teacher, has been also very faithful and active in church.

Even though I grew up with women being active in church and attended a women's university where women were taught to be leaders, the idea of women's leadership at church had rarely occurred to me. It was because of the environment of my home church where women did not play leadership roles. The church I had grown up in belongs to the Presbyterian Church in Korea (*Hahb-Dong*), one of three big Presbyterian denominations in Korea.[3] While the other two Presbyterian denominations have ordained women recently,[4] my home church has never permitted women's ordination. I had never seen an ordained woman pastor preaching or leading worship in Korea. I had never met ordained women elders participating in decision making, although about seventy percent of the congregation is women. Besides home visitations, most Presbyterian women's activities were focused on serving in the kitchen and preparing for a fellowship lunch or bazaar. Growing up in this church environment may have affected my self-identity as a churchwoman. At this moment, many women seminary students and M.Div. graduates of my home church are crying out for women's ordination with tears and prayer.

## Challenges in My Ordination Journey

In contrast to my Korean home church's situation, I felt blessed to follow the ordination procedure in the Presbytery of San Francisco, and to continue with doctoral studies in religion and psychology at the Graduate Theological Union after finishing my M.Div. program. However, there were many obstacles to ordination that I needed to overcome both internally and externally. I think there are four hurdles to ordination that my Korean colleagues and I have in common.

First, there is a psychological hurdle. As mentioned above, I felt guilty and inadequate as a woman when I began my internship. In each step of the ordination process I wondered if I was headed in the right direction. Even after becoming a candidate, I deliberated for another six years before ordination. I felt I was not ready to be an ordained pastor. I found this sense of not feeling ready to be common among my female colleagues. It is quite a contrast to most male M.Div. graduates, who usually view ordination as a logical next step.

This issue is explored in contemporary women's psychology. A sense of self begins to develop through the experiences of relations with the outer world from early childhood.[5] Women psychologists argue that women develop a "self-in-relation" while men develop an "autonomous self" because the primary caretaker is usually mother as woman. For this reason women usually develop a sense of caring for others and feel inadequate and guilty in many contexts including church.[6]

The second hurdle is cultural. When I decided to attend a different church from that of my husband for my internship, I was considered "not the obedient pastor's wife." In the same way, I was considered "not a regular female *Jun-Do-Sa-Nim*"[7] when I followed the ordination process. It was not only my experience. When one of my Korean women colleagues asked the session to approve the inquiry phase during the ordination procedures, the Korean male senior pastor asked her, "Are you really going to be a pastor?" She was already an ordained elder and a M.Div. student. This question would never have been asked if she had been a male candidate.

The cultural ethos of the Korean church has been influenced by Confucianism. As in many Asian countries, Confucianism has been imbedded in Korean culture, affecting value systems and worldviews. Confucianism defines values and norms of behavior that involve a set of defined roles and mutual obligations.[8] It emphasizes hierarchical orders between king and vassal, men and women, husband and wife, and parent and child. Due to these orders, a notion of preferring a son to a daughter was popular in the traditional society. Although contemporary Korean society no longer rigidly follows these principles, the ideas persist either consciously or unconsciously even after immigration to Western society.

The third hurdle is biblical and theological interpretation regarding women's ordination. One Sunday I preached at the regular adult service as required for the internship. The senior male pastor happened to be out of town and had arranged for a woman elder to preside. He thought it would be better because the preacher was a woman. I also felt lucky to have the woman elder who was one of a few women elders in Korean churches in northern California. It was a very moving moment for me and for other women, because it was unheard of to have both a woman preacher and a woman elder leading worship on regular Sunday worship in a Korean church.

Later I learned that one male *Jun-Do-Sa-Nim* left our church because of that service. While working as an engineer, he had completed theological studies in a conservative seminary. He believed that it is "not biblical" for women to preach or lead worship and thus could not attend a church that did not follow the words of God. I felt deeply hurt by the comment. This incident threw me a big question about becoming an ordained pastor.

First Timothy 2:9–15, especially verses 11–12, is one of the Scripture passages most frequently quoted to oppose women's ordination: "Let a woman learn in silence with full submission. I permit no woman to teach or to have authority over a man; she is to keep silent." Although I had learned the socio-cultural context of this text in my New Testament class and was well versed in the feminist theological perspective, I had no opportunity to respond to his seemingly unfair comments because he left.

Finally, there is a structural hurdle. I happened to get a call from the church where I did my internship. I became the second Korean woman ordained in the PC(USA) to receive a call to parish ministry in northern California. I feel so blessed and privileged. The number of female Korean seminary students has increased during the last decade. However, most Korean churches, not big

Choi, Moon Young participates in her ordination service, with Korean clergywomen colleagues, from left: Rev. Mickie Choi; Choi, Moon Young; Rev. Unzu Lee; and Rev. Ann Rhee Menzie. (*Photo taken by Bong Jin Im, courtesy of the author.*)

enough to have associate pastors, prefer male pastors as their "solo pastor." So it is not easy for many female M.Div. graduates to have opportunities to receive a call. Outside Korean churches, they face barriers of race, language, and culture. One of my seminary colleagues came to the United States to become an ordained pastor because her denomination in Korea did not permit women's ordination at that time. Although she was looking for a call for several years after her graduation with a M.Div., she could not get a call despite all her efforts. Finally, she gave up and returned to Korea. I feel deeply sorry when I hear such stories.

## With Prayer, Love, and Encouragement

In spite of the many hurdles, there were also positive factors that brought me to be ordained. First, I think, are my mother's prayers, although she was not familiar with women pastors. There is early morning prayer worship in Korea, so every day at five o'clock, my mother prays in front of the cross. As a child, I usually woke up to the rustle of my mother returning from the early morning prayer service and preparing breakfast for our family. For me, my mother's prayer is an emblem of unconditional love and unshaken faith in God. Once she understood my intention to be an ordained pastor, she wholeheartedly kept praying for her daughter's journey, one that has been less traveled by women.

Second has been my husband's emotional support. As a student couple, we were always busy studying and writing papers. We shared our difficult financial times together as students. Although sometimes we argued over the matters of housekeeping or financial issues, my husband never underrated my study or ministry. He always encouraged me to go further. The first semester of my M.Div. program was especially difficult. Unable to understand English perfectly and overwhelmed by lots of papers, I really wished to give up or to defer studying. One day, my husband bought a framed poem entitled "Don't quit." Whenever I was tempted to give up my studies, that picture reminded me to "never give up."

Third, there was encouragement from the congregation. I, as the first woman intern student, received much positive feedback from the church in general. When I received a call, both the supervisor of internship and the head of staff were male pastors, who had graduated from quite conservative seminaries in Korea, which did not ordain women. However, they were used to Western culture and value systems in the United States, and they fully supported my internship and ministry. I feel blessed to have met these pastors and also elders who encouraged me in many ways. Furthermore, some women church members recognized the importance of women's leadership in church. Their encouragement ignited my hope to be ordained. I will never forget their prayers, love, and emotional and financial support.

Finally, there was the solidarity of Korean American clergywomen in the PC(USA). When I attended the Korean American clergywomen annual conference for the first time in 1993, there were three ordained women pastors and a few candidates.[9] Once we met, we easily felt solidarity as Korean American women, pastors or pastors-to-be. We stayed up all night sharing our joys and despair, as well as the fruits and pains of our ministry and lives. Although I could not see them frequently, their existence as pioneers gave me encouragement and strength. I was honored to have some of them in my ordination/ installation service on April 2, 2000. They were Rev. Dr. Unzu Lee (currently Presbyterian Women's Associate for Racial Ethnic Support at Women's Ministries at General Assembly), Rev. Dr. Mickie Choi (previous moderator of the Synod of Southern California and Hawaii and currently solo pastor of New Life Community church in Los Angeles), and Rev. Ann Rhee Menzie (currently director of *Shimtuh*:[10] Korean Domestic Violence program in Northern California). In addition to preaching, leading worship, and presenting the charge, they helped me to put on the robe after laying hands on me. And they even sang a song entitled "Prayer to Friends":

> To this day I bring my life
>    born of hope, born of sand
> Yearning joy where now there's strife
>    all I have, all I am
>
> Help me to see what I must see
> Help me to be where I must be
> Restless faith abide til all are free
> Fill my life, turn my hand[11]

Many women were overcome with joy and tears while they were singing. I was crying too, letting my burdens born of sand, mistakes, pain, shame, and sorrow flow out of me and accepting the new stream flowing into me—a stream born of hope, joy, peace, and life-giving Spirit.

## Lifting Up Hands and Holding Hands Together

"Associate Pastor of Christian Education and Pastoral Counseling" is my official title at Contra Costa Korean Presbyterian Church.[12] I direct English church school for the second generation on Sunday as well as the entire weekend program.[13] I have also provided bilingual pastoral counseling services for the whole congregation and community, since I enrolled and completed the pastoral counseling training program at Lloyd Center, an accredited service center and training program of the American Association of Pastoral Counselors.

Why Christian education and pastoral counseling together? Most Korean American families consist of Korean-speaking first generation and English-speaking second or 1.5 generation members. There are also interracial marriage couples where both Korean and English are spoken. In most Korean American families, there are two languages, cultures, generations, and, at times, races. Many families face intergenerational, intercultural, and interracial conflicts. And, many second and 1.5 generation members go through self-identity crises. Korean Americans as a minority must also confront the larger American society.[14] Through Christian education, I help the second generation grow in the words of God and cultivate healthy self-identity as God's children, with pride in both American and Korean heritages. With counseling services, I help to heal the wounded hearts, to guide the wandering souls, and to reconcile the broken relationships between generations, cultures, and races. Connecting Christian education with pastoral counseling, my ministry focuses on helping Korean American Christians become holistic in faith. Looking back on the difficult experience in Princeton, I find myself doing what I hoped for then. My dream has come true in God's providence and guidance!

It was during my first communion service that I realized I had become an ordained pastor. Although I had led many worship services before I became ordained, I had never been in charge of celebrating communion. My first communion happened to be in the annual conference of Korean Presbyterian Women of Pacific Synod where I was the guest preacher. Wearing a white robe, preaching, and leading communion for the Presbyterian women's gathering was a wonderful confirmation of me as a pastor.

## Where Is Rev. Choi, By the Way?

My church has grown a lot in numbers since I was ordained, and we have three services on Sunday. Newcomers often do not know I am an ordained pastor. Furthermore, my first name is gender neutral rather than feminine. When I am introduced to them as "Rev. Choi" by an usher, they often reply, "Are you Rev. Choi's wife?" Or sometimes they ask me, after first being told that I am Rev. Choi and even after talking with me for a while, "Where is Rev. Choi, by the way?" When I repeat that I am indeed the Rev. Choi, they usually respond with widened eyes, "I have never met a woman pastor in my life" or "I did not know a woman can also be a pastor." In these times, I realize there are not many spaces where women's leadership is visible and influential in the Korean church context even after ordination. I find my role and identity as a woman pastor often serves to educate these new members and the congregation to understand women's leadership in church.

I think there are several reasons for not recognizing women as church leaders in the Korean church context. First, there are not many ordained Korean women pastors entering or remaining in parish ministry in comparison with Korean male pastors. Research finds that "female clergy are more likely to end up in secular work, interim positions, specialized ministries, chaplaincies in secular institutions, and non-parish ministries than their male colleagues."[15] One of the reasons is "the resistance to female pastors within the congregations."[16]

Second, Korean women pastors usually play roles as assistants even inside parish ministry. Most ordained Korean women pastors serve in Christian education or in English ministry as an associate pastor. It is rare for women to find a call of solo pastor or head of staff. Women pastors rarely have opportunities to develop their leadership roles inside the parish setting and thus have limited roles in transforming both the church as institution and the lives of members in Korean churches.

Third, there are few role models of women pastors in Korean parish ministry. The traditional pastoral role model is male, authoritative, hierarchical, and charismatic. Women pastors find that they are not comfortable with this tradition. At the same time, the congregation is not familiar with expectations for women pastors. It is also similar in the American mainstream churches in general. Research on women pastors shows that many laypeople identify the role of the pastor with that of a male leader and that women pastors struggle against these expectations.[17]

My colleagues and I are the first generation of Korean/Korean American clergywomen in the Presbyterian churches due to the relatively short history of women's ordination. One positive role as the pioneer group is our presence as women pastors. In relation to the patterns of laypeople's attitudes, research shows that exposure to a woman pastor in her formal role tends to increase positive attitudes toward a woman pastor.[18] I have experienced it. Once both men and women church members have listened to my sermon or participated in a communion service that I led, they appreciate my ministry. Furthermore, there are particular strengths that women pastors bring to particular areas of ministry, such as pastoral counseling. Most of the counselees are women and second generation. They often tell me they feel more comfortable sharing their personal and family problems with me because I am a woman. At these times, I feel more accepted and welcomed as a pastor.

Beyond this starting contribution, I wonder how this pioneer group will reshape the ministry? How will women's leadership transform lives and the church as an institution? When I find young second generation women pastors becoming more visible and active in Korean churches, I can see a seed of hope.

## New Paradigm: Dreaming of *Sack-Dong* Ministry

Eight years ago, my daughter was born to us in our fourteenth year of marriage as God's gracious gift, after we had given up the hope of having a child. I pray that my daughter will grow up in faith with a sense of pride in her Korean identity. As a symbol of Korean heritage and her grandmothers' faith, I presented *Sack-Dong* clothes to her. *Sack-Dong* is Korean, traditional, rainbow-striped cloth. A Korean daughter would have worn *Sack-Dong* clothes once in her lifetime. With many bright colors equally beautifully shining, *Sack-Dong* clothes remind me of equality, harmony, diversity in unity, inclusiveness, and celebration.

Some Korean clergywomen make stoles out of *Sack-Dong*. I received one as my ordination present, and my Korean clergywomen colleagues wore the *Sack-Dong* stoles in my ordination/installation service. In these stoles I see a new paradigm of women's ministry in the Korean church context: *Sack-Dong* ministry. In contrast to the traditional hierarchical male-pastor-centered ministry in the Korean church context, *Sack-Dong* ministry is one that represents equality, harmony, diversity in unity, inclusiveness, and celebration. I dream of the ministry toward God's kingdom with these beautiful stripes: equality between women and men in partnership; harmony with both the ordained and laity; diversity of different cultures, races, generations, and perspectives in Christ; inclusiveness of the marginalized; and celebration of women's gift in ministry. In fact, *Sack-Dong* ministry as a new paradigm for women's ministry is nothing but the ministry of Jesus, welcoming children and women, accepting the sick and the poor, and embracing the sinners and the weak. I look forward to seeing these bright colors of *Sack-Dong* shining beautifully in my daughter's generation.

Chapter 7

# Headlines of the Struggle

## A History by Barbara A. Roche

*Barbara A. Roche was ordained as ruling elder in 1968 and as minister of the Word and Sacrament in 1974. She was editor of* Concern *and* Horizons *magazines and dean of students at Pacific School of Religion, and she was area representative of the Commission on Ecumenical Mission and Relations of the UPCUSA.*

The Reverend Barbara A. Roche (*Courtesy of the author.*)

Let your women keep silence in the churches: for it is not permitted unto them to speak; but they are commanded to be under obedience, as also saith the law. And if they will learn any thing, let them ask their husbands at home: for it is a shame for women to speak in the church.

(1 Cor. 14:34–35 KJV)

Let the women learn in silence with all subjection. But I suffer not a woman to teach, nor to usurp authority over the man, but to be in silence.

(1 Tim. 2:11–12 KJV)

There is neither Jew nor Greek, there is neither bond nor free, there is neither male nor female: for ye are all one in Christ Jesus.

(Gal. 3:28 KJV)

For wherever we find the word of God purely preached and heard, and the sacraments administered according to the institution of Christ, there, it is not to be doubted, is a Church of God.

(John Calvin, *Institutes* 4.1.9)

*F*rom the time that the first Presbyterian congregation in America was formed in Southampton, Long Island, New York, in 1640, until the year 1964—nearly 325 years—women in the Presbyterian Church functioned without full ecclesiastical status. The cultural expectation for women, reinforced by the teachings of the church, was to be silent in public, subordinate to men, and submissive to male authority. Yet along the way there were always women who were called out by the Holy Spirit and who acted on that call despite the prohibitions.

As the years progressed, the Presbyterian Church resisted, argued, debated, moved away from a literal interpretation of Scripture, voted many times, and slowly changed to fully accept women into the ordained offices of the church.[1] Here are some headlines from the history of that long struggle.

## 1832—"Pastoral Letter" Defines a Woman's Place

In the nineteenth century, the Northeast was settled and becoming industrialized, the South was agrarian with huge numbers of enslaved persons, the Midwest was being surveyed and settled with farms and towns, the West was being opened to mining and ranching, and indigenous peoples were being relocated and decimated. Midway through the century, states seceded from the union, plunging the nation into a devastating war. The enslaved were emancipated. Reunion and reconstruction began. Women, who had been forced into nontraditional roles during the war, continued to assume more responsibility. Formal education for black persons began. Colleges opened for women. Women initiated social and political reforms. And churchwomen assumed responsibility for mission to freed persons, Native Americans, Appalachian whites, Mormons, and persons in other lands.

In 1832 the General Assembly of the Presbyterian Church in the U.S.A. sent a pastoral letter to the churches concerning disorderly behavior at religious revivals. In part, it addressed the practice of itinerant women urging women to pray in public. The letter advised, "Meetings of pious women by themselves, for conversation and prayer, whenever they can conveniently be held, we entirely approve. But let not the inspired prohibitions of the great apostle of the Gentiles, as found in his epistles to the Corinthians and to Timothy, be violated. To teach and exhort, or to lead in prayer, in public and promiscuous assemblies, is clearly forbidden to women in the Holy Oracles."[2] For the next 130 years this oft-quoted statement guided General Assembly decisions concerning women.

## 1877—Presbyterians Prohibit Women to Speak in Public

In 1872 Sarah F. Smiley—a Quaker and gifted preacher—at the invitation of the pastor, preached at the 1,400-member Lafayette Presbyterian Church in Brooklyn. The members did not object, but the Presbytery of Brooklyn asked the church to comply with the understanding that women were not to speak. The presbytery asked the 1872 General Assembly (PCUSA) to deliver and transmit rules to forbid the licensure, ordination, teaching, and preaching of women. The General Assembly felt no need to change the constitution, but reinforced the 1832 pastoral letter. On two other occasions Smiley was invited to speak from the pulpit, once at Second Presbyterian Church in Geneva, New York, and again at Lafayette, which the presbytery chastised.[3]

The opposition to women speaking in churches was intense as seen in an event involving the Woman's Christian Temperance Union (WCTU), which was founded in 1874 to educate the public about the harmful effects of alcohol on persons and society. The WCTU appealed especially to midwesterners who knew first-hand the results of alcohol abuse on farm families. It advocated abstinence and was supported by a vast number of Presbyterians. Furthermore, it generated a group of women speakers who were frequently invited into churches.

During an 1876 WCTU meeting in Newark, New Jersey, the Rev. Isaac M. See of Wickliffe Presbyterian Church invited two women attending the meeting to speak at Sunday services. The pastor of Third Presbyterian Church, the Rev. Elijah Craven, charged See with "disobedience to the divinely enacted ordinance in reference to the public speaking and teaching of women in the churches, as recorded in 1 Cor. 14:33–37 and 1 Tim. 2:11–13."[4] An ecclesiastical trial followed in Newark Presbytery, lasting several months. At one point, Craven spoke for four hours: "There exists a created subordination; a divinely arranged and appointed subordination of woman as woman to man as man. . . . It is not allowed [for] woman to speak in the church. Man's place is on the platform. It is positively base for a woman to speak in the pulpit; it is base in the sight of Jehovah."[5] In turn, See argued that what Paul said to the Corinthians applied to Corinth, not to Newark.

On January 3, 1877, the presbytery sustained Craven. See appealed to the Synod of New Jersey, which gave a slight opening to women by its decision not to sustain the complaint of Craven or the appeal of See. Not satisfied, See carried the appeal to the General Assembly, which found that the proceedings of the synod should not be reversed. All three judicatories lauded the women for their Christian evangelization and benevolence.

## 1879—Annie Bidwell Takes Exception to the Prohibitions

"They feel that I am their pastor and they will not concede that they have any other," wrote Annie Kennedy Bidwell about her relationship with the Mechoopda Indians. Mrs. Bidwell arrived in California from Washington, DC, in 1868 as the bride of John Bidwell, a member of Congress, the owner of Rancho Arroyo Chico in the northern part of the state, and a Civil War general. He had befriended and protected this small band of Indians. Over a period of years Mrs. Bidwell established a school for the Mechoopda, taught the women how to sew, and through her teaching and prayers introduced them to the Christian faith. She also initiated the establishment of the Presbyterian Church in Chico, today known as Bidwell Memorial. The Mechoopda Indians, however, did not feel comfortable in the Chico Church. At their request General Bidwell built a chapel for them. But who was to be the pastor of this church?

Mrs. Bidwell knew the biblical admonitions and the "customs" of the Presbyterian Church. Yet faced with a group of indigenous people wanting to be baptized, exhorted, and buried within the Christian community, she had to sort out what her beloved church proscribed for her in contrast to what her relationship with the Holy Ghost led her to believe.

> I have not baptized many because I do not wish to seem antagonistic to customs. But I had taken that work up contrary to customs, for at that time in our church, no woman dared to pray in public, that I knew of, and when . . . I had to assume charge, I thought I would call it Sunday School, . . . even if it was church, when it seemed to me God said to me, "Will you lie to the Holy Ghost? This is a church." I thought it was a question between God and myself and not what others thought, so with many tears, I took charge of the little church. I have often wept all the way from my home to the little church because I did not think it was proper that I, a woman, should teach men,

especially Indians whom, I thought, had less regard for women than white men. So ignorant are we. From that day to this the men have stood by me to such an extent as to be the marvel of those who attend the service.[6]

Various documents state that Mrs. Bidwell was ordained or that she was authorized by the church to be a pastor to the Indians. The minutes of Sacramento Presbytery and of the Board of Home Missions provide no supportive evidence for this claim. However, according to her biographer, "In 1879 Annie Bidwell sought advice from a prominent Presbyterian pastor in San Francisco and was told that it was within the power of her own 'session,' the governing body of the Chico Presbyterian Church, to grant such authority."[7] By all accounts her status was never challenged in the courts of the church. She died in 1918 and is still honored by the community of Chico.

## 1870–1892—The Deaconess Experiment

The good work of women like Annie Bidwell could not be denied. It seemed women were capable of assuming all kinds of responsibilities for proclaiming the gospel and doing them well. This prompted debates about the propriety of opening the diaconite to women. The 1878 General Assembly of the United Presbyterian Church of North America decided,

> That while [it] does not find in Scripture sufficient authority for the ordination of women to the office of Deacon, it is convinced that pious women may, with profit to themselves, and with great advantage to the cause of suffering humanity and of Christ, be organized to act as assistants of the Deacon; it being understood, however, that those, so devoting themselves and banded together, shall not be formed into sisterhoods living apart from ordinary society after the manner of certain Popish devotees.[8]

In 1892 the PCUSA assembly also approved the ministry of deaconesses who were elected by congregations, trained by the presbytery, but not ordained. They were to care for the poor, the sick, widows, and orphans, and many did so as nurses, social workers, and young people leaders. They wore a special garb. In the end very few Presbyterian women were attracted to this avenue of service.[9]

## 1906—Church Ordains Women Deacons

Presbyteries in the United Presbyterian Church of North America (UPNA) could designate women as lay evangelists. Perhaps their performance and the fine service of deaconesses quieted the opposition to ordaining women to the office of deacon. Furthermore, there was biblical precedent; deacons would not be voting members of a session; and it was thought that by nature women were nurturing and caring persons.

In 1906, by a large majority, the church approved an overture that asked, "Shall female members of the Church be eligible to the office of Deacon?" Of the 907 votes cast by the presbyteries, 792 were in favor and 115 opposed.

Now the UPNA found itself asking, What next? Women were Sunday school teachers, missionaries, deaconesses, evangelists, and now deacons. The National Women's Society, established in 1871 with the approval of the General Assembly, and the Women's General Missionary Society, founded in 1883, provided avenues for women to initiate mission work, speak, travel, publish, raise funds, recruit, and send out missionaries.

Should the doors be opened wider or closed tight? The church decided on the latter. Women were never ordained as elders and ministers in the UPNA. A request in 1920 was rejected,[10] and the General Assembly overturned the ordination of Elizabeth Brinton Clarke by Cedar Rapids Presbytery in 1943. She was seeking an appointment as chaplain to the Women's Auxiliary Army Corps.[11] In 1958 the UPNA united with the PCUSA, which was by then ordaining women to all offices.

## 1913—Listing Ends Twenty-four-year Dispute over Woosley Ordination

The Cumberland Presbyterian Church led the way in ordaining women, and it did so in reverse order from other Presbyterian churches. A woman was ordained to the ministry in 1889. In 1892 women elders were ordained. Women deacons were ordained in 1921—also the year that the ordination of women as ministers was finally settled.[12]

Louisa L. Woosley was born in Millwood, Kentucky, in 1862. At age twelve, she accepted Jesus during a revival meeting. Shortly afterwards she felt called to preach. Young and poorly educated, she resisted the call. She married Curtis S. Woosley while still in her teens and hoped he would become a minister so she could fulfill her calling as a minister's wife. This did not happen. She had two children and during the serious illness of her daughter prayed for her recovery, promising God she would consider the call to preach. But with the returning health of her daughter and fearing her husband would object, she put off the call. Then at age twenty-three she had a complete emotional and physical collapse. For six months she was confined to bed and during this time she prayed, searched Scriptures, and finally promised God she would become a preacher. The opportunity came two years later when the minister did not appear for the evening service. She was so gifted the elders presented her name to Nolin Presbytery to be a candidate for the ministry. At first the presbytery licensed her to preach, but then in 1889 it ordained her.

There was opposition, even from her father. In 1890 the Synod of Kentucky declared that the presbytery had no authority to ordain her, but it did not rescind her ordination. The presbytery, defying the synod, sent her as an alternate commissioner to General Assembly, and in response the synod annulled her election and directed the presbytery to remove her from its rolls. The presbytery, believing it was the final arbiter of who should be ordained, once again defied the synod and sent Mrs. Woosley to the 1894 General Assembly—this time as a commissioner. Once again her credentials were questioned, and the commissioners debated her status. The assembly endorsed her as a lay evangelist and praised her work, but it refused to seat her, ruling that she was not a regularly ordained minister.

In 1913, Louisa L. Woosley was finally listed on the General Assembly roll of ministers in the Cumberland Presbyterian Church.[13]

## 1929—Vote Culminates a Decade of Unrest

In 1919, three presbyteries of the PCUSA submitted overtures to the General Assembly concerning the status of women. One asked for ordination of women as ministers and elders; the second, for ordination of women as elders only; and the third, for an investigation into the possibility of enlarging opportunities for women in the church. The assembly took no action but did ask for a study of women's position in the church to be reported on at the next assembly. In selecting a committee, the two women appointed to serve were disallowed because only ministers and elders could serve on committees of the General Assembly.

The study went forward. The committee reported it had found that Scriptures do not forbid either women elders or women preachers; that other Reformed denominations supported women elders but on the whole were opposed to women being ministers; and finally that 60 percent of male leaders in the church favored ordaining women as elders and that an even larger percentage of women supported the right of ordination as both elders and ministers.[14] As a result, the General Assembly sent an overture to the presbyteries asking if the constitution should be amended to admit "properly qualified and elected women to ordination as Ruling Elders? . . ."[15]

The overture provoked enormous discussion. In *The Presbyterian* one minister worried, "Make his session a woman's organization, or put women into it, and you leave the minister and the church without the virile power of the men of the church."[16] Several editorials in *The Presbyterian* expressed a definite point of view:

> The question of woman is one of the most pivotal questions in the human race and in the Holy Catholic church. Error here has caused the collapse of civilizations, and may mean the apostasy of the church. . . . With all the honor and dignity, equality and exalted service appointed to woman, our Lord did not appoint one woman to be an apostle, and neither in the Old Testament nor in the New Testament is there a single case of ordination of woman either by anointing with oil or the laying on of hands.[17]

Prominent clergy and professors opposed the overture. No men of similar ecclesiastical status expressed themselves in favor, and the leadership of the two women's boards was quiet. The overture was defeated by a margin of thirteen presbyteries.[18] It was 1921—a year after the Nineteenth Amendment to the U.S. Constitution was passed, granting the vote to women.

At this time, women suffered a major setback on another front. Worried about inefficiency, the 1920 General Assembly took action, without consulting the women and without their vote, to unite their six mission boards into the Woman's Board of Foreign Missions. These boards had come into existence during the last half of the 1800s. Earlier in the century Presbyterian women had formed societies with names that seem quaint today: the Female Home Missionary Society, Female Cent Society, Female Praying Society, and so on.[19] After the Civil War, women organized these mission efforts into six regional boards: New York City, Philadelphia, Chicago, San Francisco, St. Louis, and Portland, Oregon.[20] From these locations women engaged in raising money, educating themselves about the needs in places abroad and within this country, and sending persons to places far and near to establish schools, hospitals, and social programs all in the name of Christ. The women traveled, made speeches, raised large amounts of money, and developed their own literature. Mission was personal, not abstract, and genuine affection developed among all involved.

Three years later, in 1923, the General Assembly acted in a similar manner to merge the Woman's Board of Home Missions (organized in 1878) with the Board of National Missions and likewise the Woman's Board of Foreign Missions with the Board of Foreign Missions. At this time 6,554 women's local missionary organizations existed in the church. Their giving amounted annually to three million 1920 dollars. "The sum total of their gifts during half a century having amounted to about $45,000,000."[21]

The women were dismayed by these injustices. They realized that without ecclesiastical status, without voice and vote, which could only come by being ordained, they were powerless when decisions about their institutions were made. M. Katharine Bennett and Margaret Hodge wrote in *The Presbyterian Banner* that "many (women) deplored the loss of the more intimate relations with their own Boards which had been their sole responsibility and whose members they elected."[22]

In the 1920s, the church was in turmoil over matters of theological and biblical importance. The modernist versus fundamentalist controversy was engaging not just the church but the country. Fearing a schism, the moderator of the 1925 General Assembly, Charles Erdman, proposed a study commission to discover the causes of unrest in the church. Among the many causes of unrest, tucked in at the end of its report, the commission wrote, "Lastly, there are many women in the Church who are not satisfied with present administrative conditions. Some of them fear the loss of the organizations through which they have worked so long. Some regard as unjust the lack of representation of women in the Church."[23]

As a result, the General Assembly referred the subject to the General Council for study and recommendations. The council appointed M. Katharine Bennett and Margaret E. Hodge, former top leaders of the once existing Woman's Boards of Foreign Missions and Home Missions, respectively, to investigate the causes of unrest. Reflecting on their exhaustive report, Mrs. Bennett summed it up in *The Presbyterian Banner*: "The women looked about in business and professional life and saw women rapidly taking their place side by side with men, with full freedom to serve in any position for which they had the qualifications. They saw the church, which affirmed spiritual equality, lagging far behind in the practical expression of it; they saw democracy in civic work, autocracy in church administration."[24]

The report to the General Council was persuasive. Yet the council chose to move cautiously. It asked Miss Hodge, Mrs. Bennett, Stated Clerk Lewis S. Mudge, and Robert E. Speer to develop recommendations. In the process the General Council empowered them to bring fifteen women to meet with the council. In retrospect, it seems incredible that "this marked the first time in history of the PCUSA or any other American Reformed denomination that ordained male church leaders met with women specifically to discuss questions relating to gender equality in the functioning of church government."[25]

In 1929 two recommendations came from the Committee of Four. One was to grant full ecclesiastical status to women and the other to assemble a representative group of one hundred Presbyterian women to discuss their future. Subsequently, three overtures were approved by the General Assembly and sent to the presbyteries. Overture A specified ordination for ministers and ruling elders; Overture B called for ordination as ruling elders only; and Overture C provided for licensure as evangelists.[26]

As in 1920, much discussion pro and con appeared in the church press. But unlike before, the women exhibited more energy by defending their positions. And a few men in high positions openly supported the overtures. Some men organized in opposition, identifying Overture A "with radical political, social, and religious movements."[27] In the end, only Overture B passed—the ordination of women as ruling elders. The year was 1930.

While women did not achieve full status, a significant change had taken place in the 1920s during the modernist/fundamentalist controversy. The modernist position prevailed, thus moving the PCUSA away from a literal interpretation of the Bible, which in turn ended justifying a subordinate role for women in church and society.

## 1930—Wisconsin Church Ordains Woman Elder

Moderator Hugh T. Kerr, in summing up meaningful moments of the 142nd General Assembly in *The Presbyterian Magazine*, July, 1930, did not mention the ordination of women to the office of ruling elder. Apathy did not reign in the church at large, however. The first woman to be ordained an elder was Sarah L. Dickson. Years before, working as a Christian educator in Chicago, she had befriended a young boy named Richard E. Evans. He eventually became the minister of the Presbyterian Church of Wauwautosa, Wisconsin, and she, a member. He led the session and congregation to nominate and elect her shortly after the General Assembly pronounced the vote.

## 1956—Church Approves Ordination of Women Ministers

The Great Depression began in 1929, and many ministers were without a parish. The impetus for women clergy was depressed also, and for fifteen years the General Council of the PCUSA did not address the issue. World War II, however, like previous wars, resulted in women assuming duties previously reserved for men. The war also changed the availability of ministers to serve the church, for now there were not enough clergy as men went to war. Requests began to rise from presbyteries to General Assembly asking for the inclusion of women as ministers. An overture was passed by the presbyteries in 1946 that allowed for the category of lay preacher.[28]

The first National Meeting of the Presbyterian Women's Organization (PWO) occurred in Grand Rapids, Michigan, in 1946. The spiritual highpoint of the meeting was the arrival of the Rev. Tamaki Uemura, the first civilian permitted to leave Japan after World War II. But before her arrival, events unfolded that affected the movement for women's ordination.

In order to make her presence a visible sign of forgiveness and reconciliation, the PWO asked the General Council for permission to hold a communion service and to have Mrs. Uemura join the moderator of the General Assembly, William Lampe, in presiding at the table. She was a minister in the United Church in Japan and a graduate of Wellesley College and had done her theological studies at Edinburgh University. Even before the General Council meeting, Moderator Lampe and the Stated Clerk of the General Assembly, William B. Pugh, informed the PWO executive committee that since women were not ordained as ministers of the Word and Sacrament in the Presbyterian Church, a woman could not administer the sacraments at an assembly under church sponsorship. PWO leaders and several members of the General Council challenged this interpretation of church law. A prolonged and acrimonious debate followed. "At one point in the discussion, Pugh reportedly threw his rulebook across the room and stated that it might be hypocritical to exclude women, but in good conscience as stated clerk he had to enforce the rules as he understood them."[29] A compromise was finally reached with those who thought the Presbyterian Church had no right to question the ordination standards of the Church of Christ in Japan. A member of the General Council proposed a motion that was accepted, namely, "We record it as the unofficial view of the General Council, that it would be a calamity in this day, if arrangements could not be made whereby our Japanese friend might participate in the communion service . . . and we express our unofficial view that a way should be found whereby it can be done."[30]

Ironically, after all this maneuvering Mrs. Uemura was delayed in her travel and arrived a day after the communion service. Yet her presence not only testified to the bonds of world Christian fellowship that could not be broken by war,[31] it also motivated PWO leaders to intensify efforts in favor of ordination.

Subsequently, with Stated Clerk Pugh's concurrence and support, the General Council proposed an overture to the General Assembly that would grant ordination to women. Moderator Lampe made the proposal to the General Assembly in 1946. The overture was sent to the presbyteries. While the leadership of PWO saw its wisdom, the rank and file did not organize to support the overture. Only one article in *The Presbyterian* by Methodist theologian Georgia Harkness appeared supporting ordination.[32] Of all the overtures sent to the presbyteries in 1946–47, the ordination of women to the ministry of the Word and Sacrament was the only one that failed to pass.

In 1953 all of this was to change. Lilian Hart Alexander, a ruling elder in Third Presbyterian Church in Rochester, New York, learned that her friend's daughter, a seminary graduate, wished to be a minister but was prohibited by church law from becoming one. Unaware of the history of ordination and having been a feminist since student days at Vassar College, she thought what she was hearing was discrimination. In consultation with her session, she drew up a petition in which she wrote, "When a woman is led of God so to dedicate her life, it would be difficult to discover truly Christian grounds to deny her request."[33]

Both the session and Rochester Presbytery approved the recommendation and sent it to the General Assembly asking that it "initiate such actions as may be necessary to permit the ordination of women to the Ministry of Jesus Christ."[34] Sixty-five other presbyteries signed on before it reached the floor of the assembly.

At the time the church was considering reunion with the Presbyterian Church in the U.S. and union with the United Presbyterian Church of North America. Aware that ordination of women to the ministry might not be acceptable to these two church bodies, the General Assembly moved slowly and appointed a committee to study the matter.

The three-way union plan fell through in 1954. The committee to study the ordination of women as ministers reported in 1955 that it could see no biblical or theological reasons to deny women entry into the ministry, saw no significant policy considerations impeding ordination, and saw no ministerial functions women could not perform.[35]

Thus in 1955 the overture was sent to the presbyteries by the 166th General Assembly. This time Presbyterian women organized and openly sought the vote. PWO distributed statements supporting the overture; a series of articles appeared in their publication, *Outreach.* And a study paper was used at leadership events and training schools.

In 1956 the 167th General Assembly announced that the overture passed. These simple words were added to the constitution: "Both men and women shall be called to the office of Bishops or Pastors and Associate Pastors."

On October 24, 1956, Margaret E. Towner, a graduate of Union Theological Seminary in New York City, who had been a medical photographer at the Mayo Clinic and was now director of Christian education in Allentown, Pennsylvania, was ordained by Cayuga-Syracuse Presbytery in her home church, First Presbyterian, Syracuse. *LIFE* magazine did a five-page spread on the ordination with photos by the famed Alfred Eisenstaedt.[36]

However, there was still hesitation. A plan of union between the smaller United Presbyterian Church of North America and the PCUSA was now under way, and while the UPNA had ordained women as deacons as early as 1906, it did not favor the ordination of women as elders or ministers. To smooth the merger, executives from both churches agreed that no congregation would be forced to accept ordained women elders or ministers. Within two years, in 1958, the union was consummated. The new name was the United Presbyterian Church in the U.S.A.

## 1964—PCUS Votes Women Eligible to be Deacons, Elders, and Ministers

Even more than in other parts of the country, the agrarian South revered Scriptures, upheld traditional values for women, and resisted feminism, thought to be a northern incursion. Furthermore, the church had not resolved the modernist/fundamentalist controversy, as had the UPCUSA. In church publications, leaders warned of the perils that would happen to the church and society if women were to assume roles presently held by men. Yet women were doing just that. Here, as elsewhere, speakers from the WCTU were invited into the churches. Some women were active in woman suffrage.

In 1879 the Synod of Texas asked the General Assembly of the Presbyterian Church U.S. to rule on the practice of having women preachers. The following year the General Assembly responded that "the introduction of women into our pulpits for the purpose of publicly expounding God's Word is an irregularity not to be tolerated. . . . It is the settled doctrine of our Church that women are excluded from licensure and ordination by the plain teaching of Scriptures, and therefore cannot be admitted to our pulpits as authorized preachers of the Word."[37] In 1891, 1897, and 1910 when the General Assembly was asked if women could speak in church, the 1832 pastoral letter was reiterated.[38]

Mounting pressure forced the 1916 General Assembly to appoint five men to study the scriptural teaching on women's position in the church. The report stated that women should be excluded from being ordained or licensed. It did, however, imply that women should not be prohibited from speaking in mixed groups and could be given a wider role to play in the church, a decision to be left to "the discretion of the session and to the 'enlightened consciences of our Christian women themselves.'"[39]

In 1920 the president of the Woman's Auxiliary, Hallie P. Winsborough, became the first woman given permission to address the General Assembly, but this was short-lived. The Presbytery of Concord contested her right to report. In 1925 a conservative General Assembly reaffirmed previous deliverances forbidding women to speak or pray in church meetings. It agreed that the Woman's Auxiliary might submit its report, provided a male commissioner read the report.[40]

This did not sit well with the women or with many men in the church. Protests appeared in church publications. Two sides took shape as the 1926 assembly approached. One side maintained that women joined the church on their own volition and should not object to the constitution. Another argued that it was wrong to give a narrow literal interpretation to Scriptures and said the Bible had been "used in years gone by to prove that the world was flat or that slavery was right."[41]

At the assembly, when a male commissioner rose to read "The Woman's Auxiliary Report," a commissioner moved that Mrs. Winsborough be allowed to read her own report. The assembly agreed, but the 163 to 51 vote provoked all kinds of objections, motions, counter motions, and points of order, until the assembly was recessed. The next morning Mrs. Winsborough said she preferred to have a man read the report. Before adjourning, the assembly passed a resolution that specifically permitted the superintendent of the Woman's Auxiliary to read her own report. "The Assembly cautioned, however, that 'she has a natural right to read her report to the Assembly; but this privilege does not carry any implication of membership in the Assembly or of any participation in its discussions.'"[42]

Thirty years passed before the General Assembly again dealt with the woman question. In 1955 Suwannee Presbytery asked for definitive guidance on women speaking in the church, and Granville Presbytery asked that women be allowed to be deacons and ruling elders. A study committee reported that there was no biblical reason to exclude women and requested an overture be sent to the presbyteries to allow women to be deacons and elders. After protracted debate, the 1956 assembly approved the recommendation and the overture went to the presbyteries.

The overture to ordain women as elders and deacons was defeated in 1957, but voices favoring equality for women became increasingly insistent in the years following the defeat. In 1962 the General Assembly appointed a judicial commission to recommend changes in the *Book of Church Order* to allow ordination of women at all levels. In 1963 it presented its report. Once again the assembly debated the issue before approving and sending it to the presbyteries.

This time there was a full-court press to pass the overture that read, "Both men and women shall be eligible to hold church offices."[43] *Presbyterian Outlook* carried a series of articles; the General Assembly study report was circulated; women took an active role in supporting the change; and well-known people supported the amendment. The presbyteries voted 53 in favor to 27 opposed. In 1964 women were eligible to be elected deacons, ruling elders and bishops, or pastors and associate pastors.[44]

Clara (Mrs. C.E.) Williams was elected ruling elder by the Covenant Presbyterian Church in Tuscaloosa, Alabama, on July 5, 1964.[45]

On May 12, 1965, the Presbytery of Hanover ordained Rachel Henderlite to the office of minister at All Souls Presbyterian Church in Richmond, Virginia. She held a Ph.D. from Yale University and was the director of the curriculum department of the church's *Covenant Life Curriculum*. She was also an author and ecumenical leader.[46]

## 2006—Church Celebrates Triple Ordinations

How the constitution was amended to make no distinction between women and men to serve as officers of the church is the first part of this history. The second part is what happened when congregations overcame their ignorance and fear to call women to be pastors or ruling elders or deacons. It is what happened to women who were free to speak and teach and preach, who demonstrated they could lead and moderate, and who were high spirited and self-assertive. It is what happened when women wrote theology and interpreted Scriptures. It is what happened when women and men worked together for the well being of all. And it is when the ideal took on substance that in Christ Jesus there is neither male nor female. Part two, no doubt, will also trouble us and bless us, but such are the ways of the Presbyterian Church.

# Chapter 8

# From the Baptismal Font into a Life of Service

## Melva Wilson Costen

*Melva Wilson Costen, PhD, retired in 2005 as professor of Music and Worship at the Interdenominational Theological Center. Melva chairs committees and leads music and worship for the PCUSA as well as ecumenically and internationally. She and her late husband, James H. Costen Sr., are parents of three children, six grandchildren, and two great-grandchildren.*

When a community of faith takes seriously its belief that all Christians are called by virtue of their baptism to participate in the ministry of Christ, then individual members are likely to recognize their own gifts for ministry as well as their connectedness to the Body of Christ. This has been my experience as a fourth-generation Presbyterian in a family where church activities have always been a central part of life. God's call for individuals to participate in Christ's ministry, acknowledged and celebrated in baptism, admits one to the priesthood of all believers as the first step for all other forms of ministry. I heard this concept from Sunday school teachers, church officers, and other congregational leaders throughout my life as an affirmation of the importance of the individual gifts of each member. My journey begins, therefore, at the Baptismal Font.

My birth in South Carolina might have been accidental—perhaps "appropriately" accidental, since my Mom seemed pleased to remind the family that the two of us were born in the very same room and baptized by the same pastor (often without referencing the distance of years!). Mama was summoned to Due West, SC by her stepmother who was also with child, so that Mama could be with her during the delivery of her son—my mother's brother and my uncle—nine days before my birth. Weeks later I was taken by my parents to the family church where the pastor preached, and I was taken to the font, attired in white, for a "sprinkling water bath." After words were carefully read and a laying on of the pastor's hands affirmed the empowering of the Holy Spirit, the congregation added their rousing affirmation, assuring their support. Thus began my journey toward ordination.

Both of my parents were dedicated church workers as well as public school teachers, with the latter vocation providing the only source of income. Dad was an elder, often leading activities and facilitating leadership of others, both male and female. Mother's teaching career was sandwiched between pregnancies, child births, and periods set aside for breast-feeding, each of which she managed quite well! Each day began with a gathering of the family around the breakfast table for prayer, Scripture reading (most often in memorized Bible verses by everyone capable of this form of verbal expression), a closing blessing, and finally the meal! After breakfast on weekdays the siblings who were old enough to attend classes walked with Daddy to the nearby school feeling blessed and affirmed. The day continued in school with a public assembly where prayers, songs, and religious admonitions were stressed by the principal and other adult leaders. Thus, life for our family was lived somewhat seamlessly, without a clear demarcation between sacred and secular.

I remember following my Dad to his classroom—the chemistry lab—where he taught high school students. I sat at the back of the classroom perched on a low stool or in a chair drawing pictures, painting, coloring, or browsing preschool books. I was four years old, and Mama was busy enough at home with the two-year-old and the new baby! Years later, my memory was jogged by my first-grade teacher who explained how I "graduated" from the chemistry lab to the first grade. When she heard that Professor Wilson (my dad) was babysitting his four-year-old daughter, she asked his permission to allow me to come to her classroom where students were closer to my age. At the end of the year my test scores warranted my promotion to the second grade. No one explained how I was hastily enrolled so the promotion could be validated!

Saturdays were filled with lots of diversions, but the dominant image of Saturday in my memory is the time spent in preparation for Sunday. Since Mama was always quite busy with washing, ironing, and nurturing, the siblings learned early how to clean and polish "Sunday" shoes and to place our church clothes in a convenient location so that we would not be late for Sunday school and worship services. We learned early in life that "giving our best to the Master" also meant best in appearance, brains, talent, and time, even before we could give of our own earned money. Sundays provided opportunities to interact with the extended church family—the Body of Christ—as we expressed our faith together. This day also reconnected us with the Baptismal Font and the promises that we could now make for other children in the congregation, and, in fact, the community.

This is not to say that life was uneventful, boring, or without the usual "ups and downs" experienced among siblings and friends at various age levels. There were numerous occasions to pout and attempt to "talk-back" in undertones to adults! Televisions and other technological forms of home entertainment had not been invented or were not available to families with low incomes, so there was lots of verbal interaction, naturally filled with quarrels and childhood and adolescent questions—often left unanswered. And then there was a moving day. The large, oversized truck packed with all of our furnishing and clothes announced that this was a major move.

One question that reemerges among my siblings is why our Dad left his full-time chemistry teaching career and his position as high school coach in a sizeable North Carolina city to relocate in Due West, South Carolina—an isolated, extremely small country town, far removed, we thought, from civilization! In addition to other amenities of a city, electricity and indoor plumbing were not extended into African American neighborhoods in Due West. Was this an opportunity for our parents to allow the family to experience the meaning of humility or social inequities? Or perhaps this was Dad's time to explore the innumerable challenges and solitude of country life as he pondered his own call to the ministry of Word and Sacrament.

More recently the siblings have raised yet another question that may have been foundational to the final decision: What did Mama say about the pending move? After all, she held four major positions: (1) a young mom at the beginning of her child -bearing years, already with four children (ages ten, eight, six, and four); (2) the key nurturer of the family; (3) college graduate/certified teacher, fulfilling teaching responsibilities between babies; and (4) keeper of the family, maintaining sanity within the household. Her role in matters of decision making might have been more aggressive and affirming than we are able to determine. Mama continued her quadruple roles until her death at the age of forty-one due to complications following an at-home childbirth. Then and now the family ponders deeper questions that will remain unanswered.

A few years before Mom's tragic death, Dad had accepted a call to service as a "Sunday school missionary," (later called "Mobile Ministry") in the former (northern) United Presbyterian Church. His new work required commitment, skilled leadership, talent in a variety of areas, and lots of travel. We saw in and through our dad's work the fulfillment of his call. His pursuit of the necessary requirements to be ordained to the ministry of Word and Sacrament was never abandoned. He humbly accepted his ordination to the office of elder as an appropriate way to continue his ministry, confirmed at his baptism into the community of faith. Within this context where Dad's mobile ministry put me in touch with female leadership, my own journey was gaining new momentum.

My skills and unusual talent as a musician—more specifically as an organist and a pianist, allowed me to limit myself to the role of follower rather than leader. Dad was a singer, and I, the accompanist. I learned to hide behind my gift rather than to exert myself. I had no desire to seek ordination to an office that would "cause" me to lead from up front. I was to learn early during this process that these were *my* opinions and *my* opinions only. It was Dad who, having attempted along the way to "nurture" me into new and different roles to use my potential gifts, helped to "force" me into leadership. Without prior notice, he called on me to present a report to the congregation on some of the activities in which I had engaged at a recent conference. When I shyly referred to my role as accompanist for the congregation and choir, Dad probed with direct questions that I could answer in a few words. However, my embarrassment oozed forth and overflowed with tears, to which Dad responded lovingly with the gentle reminder that "the congregation will wait until you finish crying." With much encouragement from my peers, siblings, and adults I was able to give the spontaneous report with authority!! There are some who say that this opened a Pandora's box that has never closed.

## Melva, Servant of God

My commitment to ministry as an ordained servant of God *continues* to build on this family-oriented foundation. My journey toward ordination began at birth within a particular family—a Christian family—at a particular time in history, and at a particular time in the lives of Azzie Lee Ellis Wilson and John Theodore Wilson. I accepted my call long after the moment of baptism, but all that I have described above contributed to my formation and continues even now to serve as grist for my growth and directions. Words from both parents continue to form me, and their lives serve as models for leadership and communal living. My family was by no means perfect, but it was in the context of the family that life and love and Christian journey made sense.

Family living took on a new meaning away from the familiar modes of the nuclear family headed by Mom and Dad when my life mate, James Hutten Costen, and I found each other and began to establish our own family traditions. It was a great honor to be married to a clergyman, especially Jim Costen, who possessed the enabling gifts of a leader-facilitator. He encouraged me as much as he did others in his new congregation, nudging me to assume leadership roles as often as possible. It was not helpful, however, to be surrounded by a culture that insisted on calling the preacher's wife the "first lady." This title carried with it disparaging remarks for leadership roles that might lead to ordination. Therefore, I resorted to my natural musical gift in order to remain in the background, and my natural shy mode returned to discourage any effort to "step outside the box." This explains my lack of interest in accepting the office of elder when asked by the nominating committee when Jim was no longer the pastor. I remained organist choir director and stayed in my comfort zone.

Elder Melva Wilson Costen (*Courtesy of the author.*)

## Ordination to the Office of Elder

The years 1972–1973 brought forth a variety of "firsts" in my life, reflective of times and seasons, both *kairos* (God's time) and *chronos* (chronological time). There was *kairos*—a season granting spiritual insights that moved me to a new level of understanding the power and movement of the Holy Spirit. With meditation and prayer I gradually developed freedom in discerning and relying on the Holy Spirit, trusting less the logic gleaned from printed sources. Perhaps this was my preparation to respond positively to Jim's suggestion that I should ponder carefully the request of the church's nominating committee if asked again to consider the office of elder. Jim also reminded me of the role of elder beyond the local church. He was excited about my interest in the liturgical life of the church in general and the role of music in particular. This coincided with his desire to see me become active at the national level of the church. But then there was also a chronological concern that consumed a large portion of my time. I was approaching the age of Mama's death, a time commensurate with the death of my maternal grandmother. Longevity was not a hallmark of women on my maternal side, and I had no idea at this time that this concern was also present for my oldest female sibling. As we later shared, she, too, had questioned whether she should seek a change in vocation.

The nominating committee's request came to me again early in the fall. After many hours of prayer, meditation, and study I was divinely led to say yes! My ordination took place the first Sunday of January 1973.

The day of my ordination began with telephone calls, first from my stepmother (also an elder), who apologized for her absence from the activities of the day. She also reminded me that Dad (now deceased) would be proud of me and that I would certainly feel the gentle pressure of his hand during the process of the laying on of hands. The second telephone call was from Jim, who was detained in a city 1,500 miles away due to the weather. We set a date for a special meal together in celebration of this important day in my life. The service evoked tears from my own eyes and from others who felt the power of the Spirit.

An interesting moment was my introduction to the gathered community of presbyters later that month. Following words of congratulation, someone nearby said in a whispered tone, "I thought you were already an elder since your name is so familiar." As I reflected on the words said at the ordination service just two weeks earlier, I did not remember hearing anything about familiarity of name! What did linger in my memory were the following:

- Test and affirmation of inner call—gifts for the office suitable for leadership;
- Election by the congregation
- Endorsement of all of the above by the session

Certainly it is good if the folks know your name as well.

Nevertheless it was this governing body—the presbytery—that voted for me to serve as an alternate commissioner to the General Assembly, which would meet in Omaha, Nebraska, near the end of the semester. This would necessitate my securing permission from the principal and superintendent to be excused from end-of-the-year meetings. I was notified a month before the assembly that, due to illness in his family, one of the elder commissioners would not be able to attend; and so I became an official elder commissioner. As an official delegate I was among those whose vote helped to elect Clinton Marsh as moderator (of the General Assembly of the United Presbyterian Church U.S.A.). My involvement in the Presbyterian Church locally, nationally, and internationally, began during this year, principally because of my ordination. Positions that I have held nationally since my ordination are reflective of my identity at birth and subsequent baptism as a child of God, child of the covenant, member of the Body of Christ, and uniquely African American woman in the process of becoming!

Another big event for 1973 was a change in vocation—another *kairos* moment. Perhaps it is more appropriate to refer to this change as an expansion or raising of the academic level of my vocation from elementary school to graduate teaching! My love of interacting with energetic learners and my love for the teaching profession are qualitative calls. I was already happily engaged in the teaching profession as an itinerant public school music teacher. When I was offered the position as associate professor of church music at the Interdenominational Theological Center (ITC), I turned again to extended times of prayer and meditation in search of divine guidance. In the meantime, my graduate professor of music at Georgia State University suggested that my current GPA indicated that I should rigorously pursue a PhD in music. Again the leading of the Spirit affirmed both the advanced degree and the acceptance of the contract at ITC. The fact that I was a Presbyterian elder facilitated the hiring process. The shaping of the ITC church music curriculum and subsequently a church music degree program led the way to an additional teaching assignment in Christian worship (liturgy) and later to involvement on the Presbyterian Church's discipleship and worship committee.

What then is my understanding of the call to ministry? I perceive it as a message from God communicated through the Body of Christ, which begins with life in the family. It is clear to me that family support of a member's ability to lead in general, and the subsequent preparation for church leadership specifically, are the foundations on which ordination is based:

1. The *hearing* and understanding of the call—which can take a number of years
2. The development and appreciation for *discipline,* necessary to facilitate the edification (building up) of one's own self as well as of the Body of Christ
3. Communal nurturing, which is vitally important for individuals to recognize and claim the gifts of leadership that will enable them to respond affirmatively to the call to ordained ministry
4. Strengthening and nurturing the life and faith of congregations—and governing bodies as well—which begin with positive nurturing experiences within the context of the family and move outward to the local congregation and ultimately to the larger church as a body

Of course, the greatest obstacle to one's ordination process can be, and often is, the person herself (or himself), the potential candidate. As I already indicated, this was *my* problem. I was constantly getting in my own way.

## Hope for the Future Leadership of Women

The biblical statement that "there were also women looking on from afar" (Mark 15:40) should keep us ever reminded that some women have not always been at the center of the community where decisions are made. Uncountable gifts have been lost to the community because women were not permitted to contribute their unique gifts, skills, and talents, even in the midst of the family. This should keep communities of faith ever cautious about the possible loss of talent when women who are not aggressive in affirming their call are overlooked.

There are communities that can boast about women who may not be centrally placed in church structures but are nevertheless the major decision makers from the margins. This is especially true among racial ethnic women. Where this continues to "work," women in these communities can help other groups of women find out as much as possible how they are able to manage creatively these situations. There is much mutual learning that should take place. Womanist approaches to leadership could inform and fill in some of the gaps, just as feminist ideologies can inform racial ethnic groups.

Even as we celebrate the progress women have made across the centuries and the hope it generates, women must continue to express their concerns and beware of the church slipping back into old methods of internal injustices. For every "good news" report of a woman being called by a local congregation, and the excitement of her ordination to ministry of Word and Sacrament, there are depressing reports from congregations who, even by a narrow margin, deny the possibility of calls for women. The good news from congregations celebrating ten or more years of healthy female clergy leadership is countered by two or three congregations that are anxious to remove their female clergy leadership over trivial matters.

This minimal list of examples expands like the ever-widening circles that occur when a pebble is thrown into a pond! In seeking a solution to these problems one is reminded of observations made by Paul Tillich in his discussion of three ways that the church has exercised leadership in social change: (1) through the exercise of direct political power; (2) through offering prophetic criticism, holding up before the society and its leaders the contrast between valued forms and those actually practiced; and (3) by way of silent interpretation in which change is subtly brought about by behavior and example.[1] Although each of these strategies has been used in a variety of ways to facilitate the acceptance of women in roles of leadership, the church still needs to use the second method to help fulfill the dimension of divine calling implied in the ordination of women.

Women whose pastoral skills are well honed (and continuing to be sharpened) are careful about the timing of changes in keeping with the "temperament" of the congregation. Nevertheless, they are challenged by suspicious congregants who question their motives. The slow but intentional return to noninclusive language in many of the so-called "contemporary" songs is often challenged by clergy women as well as female deacons and elders—who are then chastised by members who threaten to have them removed from their positions as pastors, Christian educators, or musicians. The backlash in the return of sexist language is reinforced by some of the recently published hymnals that many congregations are buying and using with divine language that is still male oriented.

As an active participant in justice issues in general and the rights of blacks and other racial ethnics in particular, I understand that movements exist on an ongoing continuum rather than as a before and after. I did not have the joy of marching with Martin Luther King Jr. on every civil rights march as did Jim Costen (my husband). However, with birth roots in the segregated south, I know of the duality of racial and sexist injustices before and after the "movement." Perhaps the greatest "sting" in my memory as a mother of three was the experience of subjecting two of our children to "forced entry" into the public schools of eastern North Carolina. I could not allow my six- and eight-year-old sons to see me cry as they reluctantly rode in a privately hired cab to the first integrated elementary school in the city. (For two years no taxi company in town would accept the job.) I remember the pain I experienced as my son, Craig Costen, at six years of age, became the first African American elementary school court "test case." The newspaper headlines a day after we had won the case communicated more than I wanted my sons to see. In large type the words "Craig Costen versus Rocky Mount City School System" screamed blatantly that Craig was now a "marked child." The ongoing task of helping both children live normal lives after these forced entries paved the way for others was almost more than a mother could bear! It took years of explaining to help them understand the decision and process in which they really had no choice.

## Radical Persistence and Hope

A dominant theme of the Christian faith is HOPE. Evidence of hope abounds in the narrative stories of African American Christian women, quite often combined with "defiance" or a kind of "radical persistence" that made it possible for black women to survive. With the control of their lives emanating from other than black men, some slave women, from the seventeenth century to the period of freedom, talked openly of "living in hope and trusting in the Lord." Much can be gleaned from published research on the spiritual dimensions of black women during the nineteenth century. Among the autobiographies are chronicles of the journey of the soul from damnation to salvation, as well as reflections on their (personal) true place and divine destiny in the scheme of things.[2] Women of African heritage appeared to have been quite aggressive when it came to matters of church leadership and communal healing from both the pew and the pulpit. Evidence of the hope expressed and kindled by early African American women provided the hope demonstrated in the work of black Presbyterian women into the twenty-first century. Of such is the legacy of hope—doubly strong due to the dual experience of racism and sexism—a model of hope available to all Presbyterians, to Reformed families around the world, and to the entire global church.

Women initiated and sustained strong global and national mission programs after the Civil War. Maria Fearing founded a school for girls in Congo in 1894. (*Courtesy of Presbyterian Historical Society, Presbyterian Church (U.S.A.) [Montreat, NC]. Used by permission.*)

Despite denominational disapproval, Nolin Presbytery (Cumberland Presbyterian Church) in Kentucky ordained Louisa Woosley in 1889 to be the first woman Presbyterian minister. (*Courtesy of Presbyterian Historical Society, Presbyterian Church (U.S.A.) [Philadelphia, PA]. Used by permission.*)

Annie Ellicott Kennedy Bidwell defied "custom" by serving as pastor to the Mechoopda Indians in California during the nineteenth century. (© *California State University, Chico, Meriam Library, special collections, Chico, CA 95929-0295, and Bidwell Mansion State Historic Park. This image may be protected by the copyright law of the United States [Title 17, USC]. Used by permission.*)

A backlash against women speaking in public ensued when Hallie Paxon Winsborough, president of the Women's Auxiliary of the Presbyterian Church U.S. was granted permission to present the Auxiliary's report to the 1920 Presbyterian Church U.S. General Assembly. (*Courtesy of Presbyterian Historical Society, Presbyterian Church (U.S.A.) [Philadelphia, PA]. Used by permission.*)

In the 1920s, "intrepid women" worked to remove the regulations that prevented them from participating in the decision-making bodies of the church. (*Photo from the film* These Intrepid Women, *courtesy of Presbyterian Women.*)

In the twenty-first century church, many do not even remember the days when women were excluded from decision making. Here commissioners wait in line to speak at the 2003 General Assembly in Denver, Colorado. (*Photo taken by David P. Young, courtesy of the Office of Communications, General Assembly Council, Presbyterian Church (U.S.A.).*)

Rev. Tamaki Uemura of the United Church in Japan was invited to a national gathering of Presbyterian Women in 1946. Women in the Presbyterian Church U.S.A. were outraged when the church ruled that she could not celebrate Communion because of her gender. (*Courtesy of Presbyterian Historical Society, Presbyterian Church (U.S.A.) [Philadelphia, PA]. Used by permission.*)

In 1953 Elder Lilian Hart Alexander, Third Presbyterian Church, Rochester, New York, initiated the motion that eventually led to the decision of the Presbyterian Church U.S.A. to ordain women to the ministry. (*Courtesy of Mary A. Thompson. Used by permission.*)

Margaret Ellen Towner was ordained to the ministry of Word and Sacrament by the Presbytery of Cayuga-Syracuse (New York) in 1956. (*Courtesy of Presbyterian Historical Society, Presbyterian Church (U.S.A.) [Philadelphia, PA]. Used by permission.*)

Rachel Henderlite became the first minister in the Presbyterian Church U.S. when she was ordained by the Presbytery of Hanover (Virginia) in 1965. (*Courtesy of Presbyterian Historical Society, Presbyterian Church (U.S.A.) [Philadelphia, PA]. Used by permission.*)

Throughout the twentieth century, women dedicated themselves to mutual encouragement and the development of women leaders both in the United States and around the world. Here Diana Lim and Barbara Mann worked together on the "Exchanges in Understanding" program. (*Courtesy of Presbyterian Women.*)

Caribbean and North American church women met together in 1968. (*Courtesy of Presbyterian Women.*)

Elder Lois Stair was the first woman elected moderator of a United Presbyterian Church General Assembly in 1971. (*Photo from 1972 General Assembly of UPCUSA, originally published in* A.D. *magazine, courtesy of Presbyterian Women.*)

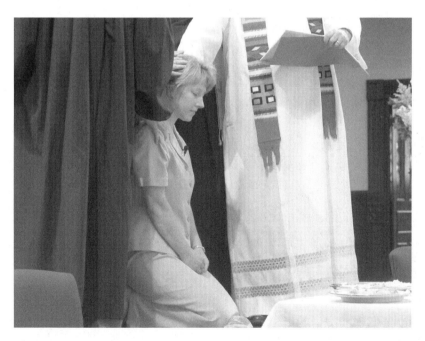

The hands of those who reach out to encourage, empower, and ordain are essential to sustaining women in leadership, such as Melissa Head at Highland Presbyterian Church, Louisville, Kentucky. (*Photo taken by David P. Young, courtesy of the Office of Communications, General Assembly Council, Presbyterian Church (U.S.A.).*)

University of Dubuque Theological Seminary especially reaches out to Native American women preparing for ministry. Here Tammy Red Owl, with mentors Henry Fawcett and Bonnie Sue Lewis, at her ordination at Valley Presbyterian Church, Bishop, California. (*Courtesy of Racial Ethnic Ministries, General Assembly Council, Presbyterian Church (U.S.A.). Used by permission.*)

Global church women bring their faith and gifts to share with the Presbyterian Church U.S.A. "Global partner" participants met at the Women's Churchwide Gathering in 2000. (*Courtesy of Presbyterian Women.*)

Chapter 9

# A Ministry Journey

## Roberta Hestenes

*Roberta Hestenes was ordained to the ministry of Word and Sacrament in 1979. She has served as professor at Fuller Seminary, president of Eastern College, senior pastor at Solana Beach Presbyterian Church, and International Minister for World Vision.*

*I*t took twenty-one years from the time of my conversion and call in January of 1958 until the service of my ordination on June 17, 1979. Twenty-one years of joy, discovery, growth, challenges, obstacles, and enormous opportunities. Twenty-one years of God's surprising grace. I remember the first date because I wrote it down in the new red Scofield Bible that I was given by Robert Seelye, the Quaker dispensationalist layman who led me into a personal relationship with Jesus Christ late one night in his home in Whittier, California. I remember the second date because it was the anniversary of my father's birthday and the night before my 6 a.m. hospitalization, surgery, and radiation treatment for stage 2 endometrial cancer. No one who knew my early family and home life or the first years of my Christian journey would ever have predicted that Sunday night service of ordination as a Presbyterian minister. It was a joyous celebration in a church filled with family, friends, and special people who had influenced my faith in significant ways. None could have seen the years of service to follow as a seminary professor, college president, senior pastor, and international leader. Only God knew all about that.

### Surprisingly and Gloriously Converted

The first and only time that I saw my parents together in church was on the night of my wedding in the small Quaker church that had pointed me to Christ and helped ground me in the faith. My father, Robert James Louis, was the youngest son in a large family of Irish Catholics who ate fish on Fridays and followed it up with generous quantities of alcohol. My mother, Rae, was the youngest daughter in a Southern Baptist family with five children. My parents made the deliberate decision to abandon both the Catholics and the Baptists and live without God or church. The accusations and hatred with which each family had attacked the other's religion left a bitter legacy of hostility to all forms of Christianity. Their decision meant that I was on my own in wondering about God. I received my first Bible in a neighborhood Child Evangelism Club by memorizing the 100th Psalm. I tried to read it, but I couldn't make much sense of it. A church bus began to come to our neighborhood, and my parents, wanting to sleep in on Sunday mornings, gave us permission to ride to the local Nazarene church, which we did for a year or so. Later a new Lutheran church was built within walking distance of our new Southern California tract home. The pastor came to call, and my parents decided that Lutheran was just enough between Catholic and Baptist that, if we wanted to, we children could walk to this church. We did.

At the age of sixteen I learned Luther's Catechism, was baptized, and joined the church. The experience of my baptism was both significant and disappointing. I didn't feel anything much during the ceremony and felt vulnerable when I walked home from the church to my poker-playing father's sarcastic taunt that I didn't look any different to him "so baptism must not amount to much." Nonetheless I learned of God, the cross of salvation, the beauty of worship, the Ten Commandments, and the Lord's Prayer and thus began my conscious journey towards faith. Still, faith in God was something I believed, not a relationship that changed my life. I was still searching, still uncertain, still spiritually hungry.

It was at Whittier College that a faculty advisor asked me, "Do you know Jesus?" I was surprised by the question, and I didn't know how to answer it. He saw my confusion and went on to share with me his recent dramatic conversion, which had moved him deeply to a joyful awareness of the personal love of God revealed in Christ. I had never thought of faith in that way, as a relationship *with* God rather than simply a belief system *about* God. I was restless all that day and eager to learn more of what this could mean for me. Later that evening, after attending a Bible study and prayer meeting at a tiny new Quaker church, Granada Heights Friends, we went to the home of Robert and Barbara Seelye, where I listened eagerly to Scripture and testimonies until I carried on my own silent, private conversation with God, opening myself up to God's love and a personal relationship if He would have me. When Robert asked me if I would like to receive Christ, I replied, "I think I just did."

So we prayed together, and I went back to my dorm room, knowing something very important had happened. And it had. I woke up the next morning with an immediate, overwhelming awareness of the reality and goodness of God. I found prayer delightful. I opened my Bible, which had been so difficult to read, and it spoke to my heart clearly over and over again. I knew that God had entered my life with grace and power, and I knew that I belonged to him. My greatest desire became to grow in Christ and to share God's saving love with others. Within weeks of my conversion, I went forward on a Sunday night after a sermon from a missionary in Borneo to offer my life in "full-time" Christian service. My life changed dramatically from those first extraordinary days, leading through many different passages to the moment years later when I stood as a pastor and seminary professor in the sanctuary of the La Cañada Presbyterian Church to take my ordination vows.

## Christian Formation

When you don't grow up in church, you gain a lot of your knowledge of the Bible and church history from old epic movies, but you need more, much more, for a lifetime of Christian service. The Christians around me knew that and began to immerse me in the Scriptures and in huge amounts of Christian reading. I had good examples, strong mentors, and a solid introduction to Scripture study, spiritual practices, exciting worship, and practice in evangelism. During my early years as a Christian, I benefited from an unusual variety of influences and traditions: outstanding preachers, great Wesley hymns, fervent gospel songs, home Bible studies, forceful American dispensationalists, winsome California Quakers, and, later, impressive Fuller Seminary professors and dynamic West Coast evangelical Presbyterians. I learned inductive Bible study methods from InterVarsity Christian Fellowship, the four spiritual laws from Campus Crusade, and was trained as a counselor in two Billy Graham crusades. These streams all led to sitting eventually as a seminary wife in the lecture halls of Fuller Theological Seminary alongside my husband of one week, John, as we prepared to serve the Lord as missionaries.

Still, I suspect, my early Christian formation was shaped not just by the abundance of teaching I sought and received but, importantly, by opportunities for ministry that were opened to me. Within days of my conversion experience, I was asked to give my "testimony" to faith in Christ to a Christian Business Men's meeting. Within weeks, I participated in a workshop on how to lead evangelistic Bible studies and began to lead a study in my dorm on the Gospel of Mark where many students either found or renewed their Christian faith. Within months I was asked to teach Sunday school. I had to learn each lesson myself before I could teach it to my fourth graders. I was challenged, stretched, loved, and given the opportunity to grow. My future ministry emerged from these opportunities.

In the small Christian Fellowship group on campus, I experienced Christian love. The home I grew up in knew a lot about sarcasm and criticism but not much about love. A primary value was often expressed as "look out for yourself; every one else is out to take advantage of you." The members of the campus CF showed me what love looked like in practice among my peers. My mother warned me against them; she assured me they were hypocrites and frauds. My father, seeing these friends one day, threw me out of the house, telling me that if I chose friends like that, I had no home with him. But, contrary to their warnings, my new Christian friends proved to be welcoming, warm, caring, and committed to each other and to me.

Once I had a serious physical problem with which my parents could or would not help. One friend offered to pay my expenses to get care. In the love I experienced in this group, in my church, and in the family of Robert and Barbara Seelye, I began to discover what kindness, goodness, and acceptance are. I was still "prickly" and sometimes suspicious of motives, but I began to learn better ways of relating to people This early experience of love in genuine Christian community profoundly influenced my life and my future ministry. Eventually it even affected my mother. My father died at age forty-two from a massive heart attack. About ten years later my mother was diagnosed with what was to be terminal lung cancer. On her deathbed, she told me that she had come to trust in Jesus largely as a result of seeing the reality of love and care expressed by my Christian friends throughout the years.

In time, I became the "prayer leader" of our campus group. This meant getting up around six o'clock most mornings to lead a small group of students praying together for the campus, the world, and each other. One of those prayers left an indelible impression. As more and more students had fresh experiences of Christ, they shared with their parents their new-found, vitalized faith. Many returned to campus with accounts of their parents' stories of similar experiences in their own youth but the dulling of faith and practice in later years. Day after day we sat on the cold seats of a small outdoor amphitheatre and earnestly, urgently, asked God to make and keep us faithful to Him all the days of our life. God has been gracious and powerful in answering those prayers. I have sought out small groups for friendship and prayer ever since.

## Double Messages

With all the encouragement to witness and serve the Lord that I received, there was also another, more confusing message. I first heard it when our church began a new college department. It was carefully explained to me that while I was obviously a leader in what God was doing among students, I could not be the president of this new group. God meant those roles for men only. While women served as officers in the Quaker fellowship, women should not serve as pastors even though the Quaker tradition suggested otherwise. At a Christian camp where I volunteered one summer, I was encouraged when I wanted to begin an evangelistic outreach ministry in a nearby resort town. But when the ministry succeeded and became an ongoing group, I was told it was not appropriate for me to be leading the weekly Bible discussions. A male should be doing this. So Scripture taught, I was told, and so I believed. I acquiesced only to watch the ministry disintegrate under the poor leadership abilities of the young man chosen to lead in my place. I began to wonder if God was really more interested in the gender of the leader than in the salvation of lost people.

I was invited to coauthor a Bible study guide for use on campuses called "Pleasing to God: The Woman God Wants." The guide provided discussion questions to study the role of women in the Bible, like Sarah, Ruth and the quiet submissive wives of Ephesians 5, 1 Peter 3, 1 Corinthians 14, and 1 Timothy 2. No Miriam, Deborah, Esther, or Priscilla! No women prophets or church leaders. In writing the study on spiritual gifts in 1 Corinthians 12, the questions were designed to lead to the conclusion that while all spiritual gifts were given by God and equally important to the Body of Christ, the public, verbal "up-front" gifts of prophesy and preaching were given to men while the quiet supportive gifts of helping and serving were given to women. It was several years before I began to question this traditional understanding.

## Theology Reconsidered

My theological system began to change in the early 1960s as a result of continuous Bible reading and theological study. Reading through the book of Acts in my daily devotions, I came to Acts 21:9, which says that Philip the evangelist had four unmarried daughters who prophesied. I went back and read it again. "Philip had four daughters who prophesied"? How could this be? I was thunderstruck. Women, I had been taught, could not receive the gift of prophecy or proclaim God's truth. But obviously, here, in the early church, in the Bible, women *did* have the gift of prophecy. They spoke openly in the congregation.

Then I began to study other passages on prophecy and rediscovered Peter's Pentecost sermon in Acts 2 where he announced that God was fulfilling the words of the Prophet Joel: "I will pour out my Spirit on all flesh and your sons *and your daughters* shall prophesy." I read Paul's instructions in 1 Corinthians 11 about *when*, not *if*, women prayed and prophesied.

My theology began to reshape and reform. Foundational beliefs about God, the cross, and salvation did not fundamentally change, but I discovered in a new expansive way the importance of the words and life of Jesus as central to Christian identity, theology, and behavior. The four Gospels had been deemphasized in my early formation. I asked questions: How can any theological system that ignores the teachings and earthly ministry of Jesus as described in the Gospels be adequate? How can patterns of church organization and gender roles that are much more restrictive than those exhibited in the Gospels, in Acts, and in Paul's letters be the normative pattern for all Christians? I spent more than ten years in a process of prayerfully and carefully deconstructing and reconstructing my theological foundations and understanding. In that process I came to embrace Reformed theology and became a Presbyterian. This theological heritage and perspective has provided rich resources for deepening and broadening my understanding of the Gospel in all its richness.

Becoming a Presbyterian did not resolve the issues regarding the role of women in the church. Although the national church ordained a few women ministers beginning in 1956, I had never seen, heard, or known any woman who was ordained or served as a pastor or seminary professor. There was one Presbyterian woman who was highly influential in my life although I never met her. Henrietta Mears was the director of Christian education and "Teacher" in the college department at Hollywood Presbyterian Church. In that role, and as the founder of the Forest Home Conference Center in the mountains of Southern California, and of Gospel Light publications, she had a major impact on a whole generation of young men and women after the Second World War. Many of her young students went on to become significant Christian leaders and pastors as a direct result of her influence. Miss Mears, as she was called, never sought or wanted ordination. She had all the freedom and opportunities she required to fulfill her calling in her time. But in her passionate leadership and her love for the Scriptures, for Christ, and his church, she was a powerful example of God at work through a committed woman. Key Presbyterian men who opened doors for me in ministry in my early years turned out to be mostly, although I didn't know it at the time, Henrietta's "boys." These men, none of whom believed in the ordination of women until later in life, did believe that God loved and used women in his service. They had seen God at work through Miss Mears, their beloved "Teacher."

## Pioneering

In 1964 John and I made the decision to move from Thousand Oaks, California, to Seattle, Washington, so that John could get his PhD in physiology and biophysics. Leaving Fuller after two years of study, he had finished his MA in nuclear physics and accepted a teaching post at California Lutheran College. We joined Emmanuel Presbyterian Church, where John became the elder for missions while I led a women's neighborhood Bible study as well as one among college faculty. Our three children, Joan, Eric and baby Stephen, were baptized. After years of consideration, the mission board to which we had applied turned us down. They believed that John could make a greater contribution to the cause of Christ as a university professor than as a teacher of sixth grade boys in Cartagena, Colombia. They were right, but I was devastated. How could I fulfill my strong sense of call if not through my husband? Little did I know that God had more plans for me than I had ever imagined.

Our second Sunday in Seattle, we went to University Presbyterian Church. Sitting in the balcony of that four-thousand-member congregation, we felt overwhelmed. It was too big for us, we thought; we would not come back. But senior pastor Robert Boyd Munger and his wife, Edith, invited us with our three children to dinner. That did it. We spent the next ten years at UPC. Dr. Munger invited John, the ex-seminary student, to join a new class to prepare to become an adult Bible teacher. John responded with interest but declared that he wouldn't join the class "unless Roberta could be in it too." Munger wasn't looking for a young female participant, but after prayer he graciously invited me to join. It was a major turning point in my life. He even found and paid for our babysitter. Within a few months, I was his assistant, teaching the class of twenty-five adults whenever he was away.

The first time I taught I had to hold on to the podium to keep from falling down with nervousness. By the second year I was rewriting the curriculum as well as teaching and organizing adult classes and small groups. Bob went to the all-male session for authorization to hire me as UPC's first Director of Adult Education. When elders questioned whether a young mother of three could handle employment outside the home, Bob assured them that I could. I was hired. Every year I was told that the budget was tight and I might be replaced by someone more qualified (and male), but year after year I was rehired. The salary was low, benefits were nonexistent, but the opportunities to learn and grow were enormous. The rhythms of the church year also gave time for me and my family to hike and camp in the beautiful forests and mountains of the Pacific Northwest.

I spent the next eight years growing in my ministry skills, juggling the multiple needs of three young children and a demanding job. The ministry flourished. My own teaching improved and met with a strong positive response. Wonderful elders and a great small group of couples provided the encouragement and support that kept us going through those challenging years. One spring, late in my tenure, the pastoral staff was planning the summer preaching schedule. One of the men said, "Isn't it time that Roberta took a turn preaching?" I held my breath with desire and dread all mixed together. When they asked me, I swallowed hard and said, "Yes." I had never taken a speech class; I had never preached a sermon. The church had never heard a woman preach. My first sermon was given in the multiple services of that enormous church and broadcast over radio. It was a very large stage for a nervous first-time preacher. By the grace of God, it went well! I have been preaching ever since. Over the years most people have responded positively, but there have always been a few that were negative, some refusing to accept a woman preacher. Attacks and criticisms are painful, but I see them as part of the territory to be learned from and endured.

Two events marked major turning points in my faith during those years. The first was the death of Martin Luther King Jr. The second was the rise of the women's movement. When Dr. King died, Dr. Munger quickly brought the staff together to redesign our worship service to reflect this terrible event. As a university church located one block from the University of Washington, we were much affected by the turmoil of the 1960s. One of our pastors had marched with Dr. King in Selma. A few in our church thought he was a communist sympathizer. John and I had taken a young black girl from the streets of the lower East Side in New York into our home when she needed a place to live. Through her, we had begun to see the world from a different perspective and began to understand the realities of poverty and race with the biblical call for justice. When Dr. King was shot, we were so disturbed that for the first time in our lives, we put on black arm bands and marched in the streets in protest of this evil. A Head Start program began in the building where my office was located. My two blonde boys were the only white children in that classroom. Later, we made the decision to enroll our children in new programs of integration in inner-city schools. I came to a deep conviction that fighting against racism and poverty and working for justice is a basic and essential component of faithful discipleship. I struggle to live this out and do it imperfectly, but a passion and burden to work for justice has stayed with me.

The second turning point was less dramatic but no less life-changing. In the early 1970s I became aware of the changing realities for women in America. Older women I knew were beginning to consider entering or reentering the workplace and finding it difficult due to limited opportunities and low salaries. Some were forced to work by the death of a spouse. Many had children who had left the home and were wondering what they were supposed to do with the rest of their lives. I thought that the church should help women address these issues and developed a new course that I called "Women in Transition." Over two hundred women showed up. I knew something powerful was going on. I became committed to feminism and the women's movement as significant for both the culture and the church.

## Controversies

While I identified and sympathized with many of the observations and criticisms of culture and church that I heard in voices for women's liberation, I could not wholeheartedly align myself with the political agenda of the more radicalized elements of the women's movement. Equal pay for equal work? Yes, of course. Women as leaders? Of course, if they are willing and gifted. Abortion on demand? No. All life is precious to God including the life of the unborn in the womb. Who should control women's bodies? Women, themselves; not men. Should women consider abortion easily acceptable as a remedy for undesired consequences of inappropriate sexual activity? No. Should women be sent to prison for having an abortion? Never. Justice for repressed minorities? Yes, absolutely. The Bible constantly speaks of justice for all, especially the poor and oppressed. Later the issues were related to ordination for gays and lesbians. This I found not so easy.

I have found it difficult to find myself often considered too conservative for the "left" and too liberal for the "right." This is painful because I care deeply about colleagues and friends who hold different views, and I care passionately about the unity of the church. My ordination vows to "seek the peace, purity, and unity" of the church are sacred to me. Sometimes these values collide in perplexing ways. Why can't I simply align with one "side" or the "other" on these difficult issues of our time? My Reformed understanding of Scripture as the only unique and normative authority for Christian faith and practice cuts through typical party lines on many controversial issues. It took me ten years to work through what I believed Scripture taught about appropriate roles for women, adopting finally what many evangelicals thought of as a "liberal" position. Many years of study and listening on issues related to sexuality and ordination have left me in a position often labeled as "conservative" or even "homophobic" for seeking to maintain the historic practice of the universal church. Yet I remain convinced that if Scripture is not considered authoritative in its statements on sexual behavior, its authority for faith and practice in other areas is seriously eroded, if not fundamentally abandoned.

Beginning in my last years at UPC, I began to speak occasionally on some controversial issues in the church. Eventually I reluctantly became part of denominational debates on sexuality and ordination. I have tried to be biblically sound, thoughtful, loving, and prayerful in these difficult matters while acknowledging my limitations and capacity for being wrong. It has not been an easy path to walk.

## Stretching

When Fuller Theological Seminary asked me to join the faculty of the School of Theology as an instructor in speech communications in 1974, I was highly uncertain. There were no other women on the faculty, and the school was about to be embroiled in a major controversy on women's issues due to the publication of Paul King Jewett's book *Man as Male and Female*. I had only a bachelor's degree even though I had done two years of graduate study in rhetoric and public address. It was my husband John who was absolutely certain that I should take the position even though it meant moving our family and his finding new employment. He took the view that he could find suitable

Roberta Hestenes prepares to speak at her ordination service at La Cañada Presbyterian Church, La Cañada, California. (*Courtesy of the author.*)

employment in any place with a large university nearby while I, as a woman in ministry, would find opportunities much more limited. Therefore he would be flexible and move in order to support me. Wow!

The initial offer was for a six-month part-time position with no guarantees about the future. I arrived slightly late to my first faculty meeting to find all the seats filled with men, all much older and much more learned than me. After what seemed like forever, one kind man got up and offered me his chair. So it began. I started by teaching a speech class with one hundred male students. I introduced a new seminary course on "Building Christian Community through Small Groups" and one on "Women in Transition." During the arguments swirling around issues of Scripture and the roles of women, I listened to male scholars debate furiously about what women could or could not do. I vowed fiercely that no such debates would happen again at Fuller without women's voices being heard.

Thankfully, it was not long before President David Hubbard, Provost Glenn Barker, and the faculty and board of Fuller committed themselves fully to the equal ministries of women alongside of men. The number of women students grew from seventy in my first year to over seven hundred five years later. I rejoiced in the increasing numbers of women who became pastors, therapists, psychologists, or missionaries as well as in the increasing number of women brought on to the Fuller faculty. While at Fuller I began a new program in "Christian Formation and Discipleship." I also served part-time at La Cañada Presbyterian Church with Gary Demarest, finished my MDiv and DMin, received tenure, and wrote a book for Westminster Press on *Using the Bible in Groups*. The celebration of my ordination with my husband and teenaged children confirmed my ministry and opened new doors. It provided the new privilege of presiding at the Lord's Table. I have been surprised by the deep impact this has had on me and on those who have come to the Table grateful to receive communion from the hands of a woman. Giving communion has been one of the greatest privileges and sources of blessing over the years. I have thanked God many times for the grace shown me not only as a Christian but as a person called to be a Presbyterian pastor.

## Broader Influence

After ordination, while undergoing six months of cancer treatments, I received a phone call from Stan Mooneyham, the president of World Vision, a dynamic international Christian humanitarian ministry working with the poor and oppressed in the developing world. Would I be willing to join the board of World

Vision? "It is time that we have a woman," he said. I have since heard that sentence many times by those who do not realize how patronizing or condescending it can sound. But then, I heard it with joy because this was an opportunity to be involved in a world-wide Christian ministry of caring for children and families in disasters and conditions of deep poverty. My original missionary call was finally being fulfilled. What God put into my heart years before, God opened up in his time. I took my next sabbatical from Fuller in Africa, Australia, and Asia, moving among starving and dying children during the famine of Ethiopia, seeing the deep poverty among families in the garbage dumps of Egypt and the Philippines, and experiencing the wonderful vitality in the churches of the poor. I have served World Vision as an active board member and as International Minister for a total of more than twenty-five years, traveling often in the developing world. It has deepened my faith, challenged my theology, and broken my heart. It has been one of the deepest privileges and joys of my life. Serving the world-wide church as well as serving in local congregations wherever I have lived has energized me, stretched me, and kept me close to the Lord.

In 1987 I was astonished to receive an inquiry from Eastern College, an American Baptist liberal arts school in St. Davids, Pennsylvania. They asked if I would be interested in becoming president. I told John that this would be the shortest interview in history because they would ask me if I would become a Baptist. I would say, "No, I am a committed and convinced Presbyterian," and that would be that. They did ask me; I did say "no," but to my surprise they called me as president anyway! I was the first woman president in the history of the school and in the Coalition of Christian Colleges and Universities. The faculty was stunned to be introduced to their new president, who was a California Presbyterian, experienced in graduate theological education rather than the liberal arts, and a woman, to boot!

The mission of the college was "The Whole Gospel for the Whole World," which was right at the heart of my passion. I consider myself primarily a pastor and a teacher, not an administrator or fund-raiser. But with the help of many colleagues I learned. We increased the enrollment of the college three-fold, eliminated deficits, increased the percentage of African American students from 3 percent to over 20 percent, and began programs in the inner city of Philadelphia and the business schools of Russia. We founded an Institute for Christian Women in Leadership, which the Board renamed in my honor when I left after ten years. While at Eastern I also served as a parish associate at Wayne Presbyterian Church. When the senior pastor underwent treatment for cancer, I filled the pulpit for him. This rekindled my desire to serve full-time in the church, and not much later I accepted a call to become the senior pastor at Solana Beach Presbyterian Church near San Diego.

Serving as the first woman senior pastor in a church of more than two thousand members proved to be both a satisfying experience and a real challenge. The search committee took the congregation by surprise with their recommendation of a woman senior pastor. Some were wonderfully supportive, and most were positive, but a small group of core members were less enthusiastic. One leading woman brought me a plant for my office after which she announced that the church was not ready for a woman senior pastor and I should resign immediately. She never changed her mind even when our congregation was named as one of three hundred outstanding churches in America.

Unfortunately, the church had difficult issues to deal with. There were allegations and evidence of immorality on the part of the high school youth director, and then, most sadly, the awareness that the much-loved and respected previous senior pastor had been guilty of serious sexual misconduct throughout most of the years of his ministry at the church. The tensions and pressures associated with dealing with such traumatic problems took its toll. After the stated clerk of San Diego Presbytery filed charges against my predecessor, a specialist was brought in to help the congregation. It became clear that I would not be able to stay for a lengthy pastorate. I concentrated on preaching and helping the congregation to heal while it shaped a new vision for a positive future.

World Vision had been asking me for some years to join their staff as full-time Minister-at-Large, working on Christian spirituality with our 22,000 staff around the world. I finally made the decision to accept. Preaching and teaching throughout the world since that time, I continue to rejoice in the goodness of God. From my childhood to my rapidly approaching old age, I have seen the Lord's faithfulness in many ways both large and small. God has answered prayer, sometimes dramatically; given me strength; and provided the guidance I have needed. I have dreamed dreams, and God has filled them way beyond my highest hopes or wildest expectations. I can truly thank God for his salvation, mercy, and love. The way has not been easy, my limitations very real, but it has been a great journey. He is gracious to all who call on him. To that good news, I am a grateful witness.

Chapter 10

# In the Picture, in the Halls, in the Home

## Marian McClure

*Marian McClure has been the director of the Worldwide Ministries Division of the PC(USA)'s General Assembly Council since 1997. She was ordained as an elder in 1983 and as a minister of Word and Sacrament in 1996. Her previous work experience includes teaching politics at Harvard University and serving as a program officer for the Ford Foundation in Mexico City.*

*M*y ordination as an elder was just as important to me as my ordination to the ministry of Word and Sacrament. I was almost thirty years old when I was made an elder and had been worshiping at Church of the Covenant in Boston for about four years. It was the church where I'd been riveted by my first experience of hearing a woman preach. Highly dedicated to this congregation, I attended choir every Thursday and listened hungrily to the sermon every Sunday, commuting forty-five minutes each way, usually by public transport. Graduate study at Harvard made me lonely, and I drank in the camaraderie of this congregation.

Then one day I entered the fellowship hall for coffee hour and looked around for someone who needed a word of greeting or encouragement. I realized at that moment I had turned a corner from needing to receive to wanting to give. I was increasingly called on for worship leadership roles. I refused to let my penurious student's existence keep me from pledging during the stewardship drives, and it was the sweetest experience of giving I've ever had.

The session contacted me about becoming an elder. This amazed me and moved me deeply. I had academic accomplishments to my name, as did many fellow worshipers. I had often been elected to leadership in secular settings. But this was different! It was about spiritual gifts. It was an acknowledgement about who I was, not about my credentials, and about what I offered a faith community, not just any organization. It was about a charism, not just a skill. At the service of ordination and installation, when people came forward to lay hands on me, I could not have been more stirred, affirmed, and challenged.

I started seminary ten years later, after completing my doctorate and working five years for the Ford Foundation. I knew only that God wanted me to attend seminary. I did not know anything else about where this was heading. It was courageous enough just to start, because my then husband was intent on me becoming invisible, not a lamp on a hill. There was no spoken connection between my registering at Boston University School of Theology and the fact that the next day he injured me in a rage. But I've always thought it significant, the timing of that worst attack. I ended my years of efforts to save that marriage three months later, and I transferred to Louisville Seminary.

Seminary was great. I wanted to stay forever, like Peter at the transfiguration saying to Jesus, "It is well that we are here; I'll build us some tents." I grew up a preacher's daughter and at my father's urging "came under care" just in case all this was leading to the ministry of Word and Sacrament. One of the moments of discernment of a call to that ministry came during a student pastor internship. About to step into the pulpit, I took my emotional temperature by asking myself, "Are you scared?" The answer came back with a warmth and clarity I can still recall today: "No, I am not even nervous. I am Marian right now, and I've never been more Marian. And isn't God wonderful to make it possible for me to step into pulpits the rest of my life?" This from a person who was sure of only one thing when she started seminary—that it would not lead to preaching!

## In the Picture

The picture many people all around the world have of the leadership of our church is a picture that includes me. If there is anything distinctively interesting about my ordination to the ministry of Word and Sacrament, it is due to my being ordained to the work of the General Assembly Council. I now serve in the Worldwide Ministries Division, as its director. That means that I very frequently represent the denomination's mission program in public engagements of the PC(USA) and internationally.

I want to tell you about two aspects of my life as an ordained woman. The first is about having this very visible role when appearing in places where women are not in equal roles with men in church leadership. I offer you vignettes of what it has meant for me to be "in the picture"; this is your photo album too, since your representatives put me there! Then I want to tell you about the prophetic sermon preached at my service of ordination in September 1996 and how it has framed my ministry in the halls where you have placed me.

## Pakistan

I spent a year as Worldwide Ministries Division's specialist for support of educational mission before I became the division's director. During that year I went to Pakistan. When I visited the seminary in Gujranwala, I was asked to take part in the dedication of a building, a dormitory for women. I was embarrassed to be honored in this way since I had had nothing to do with this dormitory project. I learned that though our partner church there does not have a policy against ordaining women, it is not done. So the women studying at the seminary and living in this dorm were not on an ordination track. As our little group gathered in the foyer of the new building, we had a prayer and shared a liturgy, and then came the dramatic dropping of the banner covering the plaque that was to commemorate the dedication event. A passage from Psalms is inscribed on this plaque embedded in the wall, followed by the words "dedicated on this date by the Reverend Doctor Marian McClure." It dawned on me that one of the purposes in inviting me was to have that obviously feminine name preceded by those particular titles in a place where everyone could connect the plaque with the purpose of the dormitory! It was not the last time I had the sense that progressive men had made good use of my visit to their country.

## Congo

My first trip abroad as director of Worldwide Ministries included a week in the Democratic Republic of Congo. At one point I met with pastors of one of the Presbyterian denominations there, to hear what their life and ministry was like. Life is hard in Congo, and I felt privileged to hear about it. Then a somewhat shocking thing happened. There were a few women pastors present, and they suddenly started telling me that they were treated as second class by their pastor colleagues and even congregations. One of them blurted out, "We are treated like dogs." They were shushed. But they had told me what was on their hearts. Would they have spoken out had I not been a woman and a clergyperson in a leadership position? I can only pray that something good came from that moment.

Another event was at the Good Shepherd Hospital, where we always have mission coworkers assigned. Like more than 80 percent of all PC(USA) mission coworkers, they were all laypersons. They asked me to lead a communion service. I asked permission from the hospital chaplain and asked him to assist me. One missionary brought homemade bread in a Congolese basket. In the intimacy of the guesthouse living room, we shared the Lord's Supper. It was rare for this group to hear this liturgy in their mother tongue, English, and it meant a great deal to them. It meant at least as much to me. It wouldn't have happened without my ordination.

## Korea

Not long after one of our partner churches in Korea began ordaining women, there was a celebration of the anniversary of their Presbyterian women association's founding. It was good timing for my first visit to Korea. That Sunday, the pastor of a huge congregation in Seoul was kind enough to invite me to preach at the fifth service of the day. No clergywoman had ever preached in that pulpit before. I wore a traditional Korean dress, which may have sent a sort of subliminal suggestion to the congregation in reinforcement of the bold gesture the pastor had made in inviting me. I was able to contribute the love offering to me that day to a Korean woman who had gotten her denomination's nomination to attend an important international church event but who needed funding for her participation.

## Brazil

On the chance that the Presbyterian Church of Brazil (IPB) would come back into a partnership relationship with the PC(USA), I went with a delegation to that denomination's General Assembly. Some U.S.-based Presbyterian denominations that split off from ours seemed eager for reconciliation not to happen between the IPB and the PC(USA). I sought out one of those U.S. denominations' former stated clerks for a lunch at the hotel. I asked him about why his denomination does not ordain women. I listened respectfully to a discourse arguing that in the Bible there are prophets, priests, and kings (royals), and that women in the Bible are either prophets or royals but never priests. That seemed like a weak argument, given the Reformation commitment to the priesthood of all believers.

Later, on the assembly floor, the speakers who got to the mikes first made it sound like relating to the PC(USA) would somehow contaminate the IPB. But our delegation set the record straight and explained the true commitments of our denomination by explaining the symbols in the PC(USA) logo. The Holy Spirit moved hearts and minds, and many commissioners flooded onto the dais, apologizing and embracing us and promising to bring the partnership relationship up for future votes. There were only a few women in the huge sanctuary, and I was probably the only clergywoman most of commissioners had ever seen. A photographer was selling snapshots taken each day at the assembly. All the ones with me in them were sold out, and I later heard that they were posted in offices and hallways in churches around Brazil.

## The Vatican

I asked a Catholic diocesan official in Louisville to be the ecumenical delegate in the commission for my ordination. He turned me down gently, explaining that it might appear that he was approving of the ordination of a woman. It's a bit inconsistent that sometimes Catholics will participate in the ordination commission of a Presbyterian man even though he belongs to a denomination that ordains women.

My next conversation with Catholics about women came when Pope John Paul II invited the Christians of the world to advise him about how he could use his role as pope to promote Christian unity. The PC(USA) responded by establishing a two-part dialogue through the Vatican's Pontifical Council for the Promotion of Christian Unity. The first dialogue was in Louisville, and the second in the Vatican. The PC(USA) delegation included several PC(USA) women besides me, lay and clergy. The Catholic delegation was headed by a cardinal. The fascinating discussions showed no signs of ever venturing into the role of women in the church. But when the role of bishops in listening to the needs and perspectives of the whole church came up, I took a deep breath and said that no amount of listening would be as effective as including women as equals. They expressed disagreement, of course. In theory, their approach is reasonable. But our Calvinistic view of the fallen nature of all persons, including clergy, tells us that in practice if you want clergy as a collegium consistently to take account of the needs and views of women, you have to include women as members of the collegium.

## The Middle East

From what you've read so far, you may think that I was an advocate for women's ordination. But that is not true. I am of a Presbyterian generation that did not have to fight for women's ordination and therefore did not have to make a personal decision that it was worth a fight. I went through seminary without having to do real soul searching on this topic.

So it wasn't until I was advised to wear a clerical collar in the Middle East that I finally had to wrestle deeply. I think Christians have to hold ourselves to a tough test when we know our behavior may cause offense. On a three-week visit to the Middle East I would meet with Orthodox and Catholic leaders as well as Muslim and Jewish ones. Protestant clergy in the Middle East wear clerical collars most of the time, and always when meeting with their ecumenical and interfaith colleagues. So I had to ask myself this fundamental question: Is the ordination of women so essential to the gospel of Jesus Christ that to hide it would be to hide what I believe about the gospel? I really wanted not to cause offense. But I finally had to concede that "yes" is my answer to that question. The role of women in the new creation is not the role of women in fallen creation, and we are to proclaim that new creation and show it in the life of the church.

The only obvious reaction to my clerical garb by church officials came when I went to meet a famously crusty Orthodox leader. He asked on seeing me, "Have the Presbyterians run out of good men, then?" But I was undaunted, and we proceeded to have an excellent and cordial exchange of ideas on many topics.

The reaction of ordinary Christians was apparent on Reformation Sunday. I had preached that morning at the Presbyterian Church in Damascus, and there had been no time to change clothes. So in the afternoon I was climbing the steps of the ancient pilgrimage site of the Saint Tekla monastery wearing a clerical collar. A colleague who is fluent in Arabic told me, "You may have become more interesting to the other pilgrims than the site itself." As the stream of people coming down the stairs passed him he could hear them exclaiming, "*Khoury mara!*"—woman priest! I can only hope that the sight of me got them thinking about what Saint Tekla did in ministry. Converted by Paul's preaching but from a Roman family, she was chased into the desert by people intent on killing her. She lived in a cave that had water, and when people came to visit her there she healed and baptized them—*khoury mara*?!

## In the Halls

Ordination of women, or of men for that matter, would not be very important if it only boiled down to a secular view of equality, or self-actualization, or even symbolizing something for people as they go about the real living of lives. For me, the purpose of being set aside for particular ministries in the life of the church is summed up in that stylized towel we call a stole. It is about "washing feet," about putting your very life on the line in the way of Jesus Christ, to set free people who are captive to sin or injustice.

This value, this identity as an ordained person, was crystallized and given to me as a gift in the form of the sermon my brother John McClure preached at my ordination in September of 1996. Not everyone has a professor of homiletics for a brother! The text was the story of Esther and the banquets she threw in the halls of power in order to save a people facing extermination. John knew I could relate to the story of a woman's courage in relating to a dangerous spouse. But he was also calling me to acknowledge that as an insider in an agency with tens of millions of dollars, I was stepping into halls of a certain sort of power and would be able to gain the ear of people in other halls of great power. He wanted me and all others present that day to remember those outside the gates, those who need a friend on the inside who is willing to be identified with them.

Two years later, I received a call from the parent of a woman who as a child had been sexually abused by a Presbyterian missionary several decades earlier. There is a story to tell about being an "Esther" among the many courageous souls who responded to this call alongside me. It is a story that taught me about trusting survivors to know what they need and clearing the way for them to receive it. The real protagonists of the story are the women who joined that first voice, who accused the perpetrator, and then when he died cooperated with an independent committee of inquiry. For me, it was a time to use my access to the wherewithal to "throw the banquet," to convene those who needed to hear, to intervene for those

The Reverend Doctor Marian McClure (*Courtesy of the author.*)

outside the gates. In 2004 nearly a dozen amendments to the constitution of the PC(USA) were passed, all of them improving the ability of our church to respond well to survivors of abuse. These changes are among the large results from the many small acts of courage and vision along this journey. I thank God for placing me and many others where we were placed for "such a time."

Not all access to the halls of power yields such results. I led an ecumenical delegation to visit United Nations Secretary General Kofi Annan around the time the U.S. military entered Iraq. I had been briefed by our U.N. Office staff about issues related to relief work in Iraq and about the Oil for Food program run by the U.N. The concern was that the resources of Iraq should be handed over to Iraqis as soon as possible. During the meeting with the Secretary General, I did not emphasize the Oil for Food point at first. But a gracious Mr. Annan was open about his own church background, and I decided he would understand if I referred, one believer to another, to "temptation." So I took another one of those deep breaths and said, "We ask that you beware of the temptation to hold onto the oil money the U.N. is using. It belongs to Iraqis and should not be used by the U.N. longer than it has to be." Whatever happened with that money inside the halls, Mr. Annan was truly warned!

On another occasion, I wrote to a high-ranking Bush administration official, who is a Presbyterian, to warn her of perceptions by Christian leaders in many parts of the world that the United States has taken on a posture of "empire." I said that the administration needed to focus more on building justice and peace between Palestinians and Israelis. She wrote back about the road map for Middle East peace but not about the perceptions of "empire." As I write, the negative perceptions about the U.S. use of power continue to grow and to harden.

Neither of these attempts to reach into other people's halls was as effective as the attempts to be faithful in my own. That is how it is. Baptism is about entering into the way of Christ, and it involves all of us in risk taking. Ordination intensifies the responsibility to live out those baptismal vows by giving particular persons particularly visible roles. It is in our own spheres of ministry that we will have the most opportunity to live out that responsibility and witness.

## In the Home

In July of 2000, Stephen Taylor and I stood up during a Sunday morning worship service and made our wedding vows. We could not have become the happy couple we are without women's ordination. Stephen, who was raised a

Methodist, did graduate study in piano performance and church music at a Southern Baptist seminary. He was there during the time that the seminary was taken over by conservatives who make a point of restricting women's roles in church and society. Very alienated by that experience, he switched to medical studies and stopped attending church. When we started dating, right away I asked him to visit some Presbyterian churches with me. In God's providence, women preached during all of the first three services where we worshiped together. His relationship to the church was healed by these experiences.

How many people now come to Presbyterian churches in part because of women's ordination and what it says about the gospel of Jesus Christ? Perhaps many do. Perhaps that number will continue to grow as we are increasingly "in the picture" and "in the halls." This I pray.

Chapter 11

# Encounters and Visions

## Ofelia Miriam Ortega

*Ofelia Miriam Ortega is a pastor of the Presbyterian-Reformed Church in Cuba, a theological educator, and an ecumenical leader. She has served as a pastor, professor, and seminary president and worked for the World Council of Churches for a decade. Currently she is the founder-director of the Institute for Gender Studies in Cuba.*

Listen! I am standing at the door, knocking; if you hear my voice and open the door, I will come in to you and eat with you, and you with me.
(Rev. 3:20)

*I* was born in Cuba, in a poor Roman Catholic household. When I was three months old, I was baptized in the Roman Catholic Church. My mother believed in the importance of religious education, so she sent me to the church that was closest to our home.

It was a Baptist church—but an exceptional Baptist church. The pastor, who was also a medical technician, offered medical services to the poor community surrounding the church in a laboratory built onto the manse. This pastor had a great sense of humor. He received the children and young people of the neighborhood with an infectious joy that suffused the worship services, classes, and other Sunday activities.

At the age of four I began attending a Presbyterian church because the Presbyterians had the best school in the city, "La Progresiva," which allowed poor mothers to pay tuition by washing clothes for middle-class students who lived in the school dormitories.

Looking back, I realize how great an influence the ministries of these two local churches and of the school had on my life. Faith and social commitment were an essential part of my early ecumenical encounters.

## Spiritual Development: Self-affirmation, Self-direction, Self-confidence

Throughout my life, my spiritual development was closely linked with the process of developing self-affirmation, self-direction, and self-confidence. Economic and cultural factors played an important part in this process. When did I become aware of a certain devaluation of my own humanity? I remember one particular moment. Someone was visiting our home and my mother said, "It's a pity that she isn't a boy. It would be easier for her." My mother's thinking was valid: if you are poor and on top of that, a woman, your possibilities in life are limited. I crawled under my bed and cried. I felt a huge abyss open up between me and the rest of humanity. If my mother didn't love me, who ever would love me? It became more difficult for me to encounter not only my friends but God as well. Tears, loneliness, anger, and self-pity accompanied me for a long time.

Perhaps I did not pray during all those years? Yes, I prayed. But it was a desperate kind of prayer. I prayed for changes but did not have the strength to change; nor did I know what needed to change.

Finally God came to me. When God's passionate and compassionate love surrounded me, life began anew for me. I felt accepted. "This first context of being accepted is and remains for many people the most important source of faith and courage for living, and it is not difficult to see in the faces of the unhappy people who have never experienced any of this, what elementary injury their soul has sustained. And even when a woman may forget the infant at her breast—which does in fact happen among people—'yet I will not forget you,' says God through Isaiah (Isa. 49:15)."[1]

Some time ago a good friend asked me, "Are there differences between the conversion experiences of men and women?" The question surprised me. Nevertheless, upon reflecting on both my experience and that of my mother, I noted some differences.

Women's spirituality is holistic and encompasses the totality of our relationships with all of creation, our fellow human beings, society and nature, work and recreation. In other words, it includes all dimensions of life. We believe that Christian spiritual development cannot be equated only with the development of the soul, nor associated exclusively with prayer and virtue. Rather it is to be viewed as development of the whole person. Furthermore, all that limits the development of our full humanity is an obstacle to our spirituality.

Women's spirituality goes beyond autonomy to relationship. Most psychological models of human development stop with autonomy—maturity as differentiation from others, independence, and taking control of one's own life. For women, the path towards maturity includes belonging as well as inde-

Ofelia Miriam Ortega receives visitors to the Evangelical Theological Seminary in Matanzas, Cuba. (*Courtesy of David P. Young.*)

pendence. Acceptance, relationship, and belonging are all essential to our spiritual journey.

As a girl in the midst of two brothers, it was some time before I recovered from the damage done to me during my childhood and adolescence. The road toward self-confidence was a long one, taking me

> from sadness to happiness
> from frustration to hope
> from isolation to community.

Along the way, the church community was a great help. The youth group (with female leadership) and many other persons in the Presbyterian Church of Cárdenas supported me.

The experience of God's acceptance changed my life. I gained a new sense of dignity, and a process of self-affirmation began within me. I began to move towards autonomy and maturity. Immediately I decided to share my experience with others. At that moment, I was not going to school because of economic difficulties at home. Nevertheless, I promised myself that I would find a way to finish my pre-university studies so that I might study theology. I very much wanted to commit myself to the witness and mission of the church.

## Confronting Obstacles to My Vocation

After graduating from "La Progresiva" in 1956, I attended a youth conference of the Presbyterian Church, where I had a strong and decisive experience of God's call to service in the life and work of the church in Cuba.

I decided to study at the Evangelical Theological Seminary in Matanzas, Cuba. The only avenue to do so was to enroll in the School of Christian Education, since the School of Theology did not accept women as candidates for the ordained ministry. One of the pastors present during my interview asked me, "Why do want to go to seminary? You are young and attractive; you would be a good pastor's wife." I was also asked, "What will happen if you get married while you are studying?" These questions would never have been posed to a male candidate. But I was a woman, and a clear distinction was made between men and women.

I entered seminary in 1956 with a firm conviction that God would use my life according to God's own will. I finished my seminary studies in 1959, the year of the Cuban revolution. To my great surprise I was invited to teach at the seminary in 1960, due to the exodus of foreign professors. I became a professor of pastoral and Christian education as well as director of Christian education at the Presbyterian church in Cárdenas.

## Encounter with My Own Context

It was not until the decade of the 1960s, after the triumph of the Cuban revolution, that I truly encountered the realities of my own context. I found myself participating in the literacy campaign organized by the Cuban government, along with many churches and other nongovernmental organizations.

The youth and young adults of the Cárdenas Presbyterian Church went to work on the construction of a multipurpose building in a poor neighborhood called "La Arrocera." It was designed as both a house of worship and a community center where members of the community could meet to organize as well as learn to read. And we, the women, provided the leadership for this wonderful experience of participatory democracy.

This "ecumenical encounter" taught me two important lessons—concepts that I would later discover formulated with clarity in my theological studies. First of all, I learned that in order to be truly ecumenical, it is necessary "to break out of the circle of self-absorption and pay heed to the bloodied face of our fellow human beings. For they are the great sacrament of God, the signs and instruments of authentic divine reality. If we do not share life with the oppressed, we do not share life with God."[2]

Second, I experienced the reality that "Christian life, while intensely personal, is always communal. . . . The privatization of piety is not part of the Christian tradition and it undermines the Christian life. . . . Christian spirituality is, therefore, the spirituality of Christian community. But it is not Christian community lived in isolation from the world."[3]

Thus, going beyond the walls of the church to an encounter with the larger community was a fundamental part of my personal development and my theological formation.

## Search for an Adequate Theological Formation

It became clear to me that I needed further theological preparation if I were to continue teaching in Cuba in the midst of such significant changes in the society and in the church. This time my request to study in the School of Theology was granted. It required great effort to engage in my studies while continuing to serve as a commissioned Christian educator. But what joy the classes in theology and philosophy, biblical languages, and other subjects brought me! I was the first woman to receive the Bachelor of Theology degree in our seminary.

I am indebted to my professors of theology, bible, and homiletics: the Rev. Dr. Sergio Arce, the Rev. Manuel Rodríguez, and the Rev. Francisco Norniella, who always expressed confidence in my abilities while patiently guiding me. I am also grateful to Dr. Lilian Strong (Presbyterian), Elder Lois Kroehler (Presbyterian), Dr. David White (Methodist), and the Roys (Episcopalian), who worked so hard as missionaries to provide us with tools appropriate for Christian education and for pastoral ministry in our churches.

## Vocation As an Ordained Minister

Many people ask me, "Was it a struggle to get the Presbyterian Church to ordain you to the ministry of Word and Sacrament?" My answer surprises them: I never requested ordination. I was commissioned as a Christian educator in 1959 and that was my primary responsibility until 1967, when the church decided to ordain me so that I might administer the sacraments. I was ordained February 17, 1967, at the same assembly in which the Presbyterian Church in Cuba separated from the Synod of New Jersey and became an autonomous church. Nevertheless, it is important to note that local congregations offered me opportunities to preach and teach from a very early age. The pulpits in my region were familiar to me from my grade-school days. So now it was the right to administer the sacraments that was new.

I was assigned to be pastor of the Presbyterian church in Períco, while continuing my work as director of Christian education, evangelism, and stewardship of the Cuban Presbyterian Church and my tenure as professor of Christian education in the Evangelical Theological Seminary in Matanzas. Since my ordination I have been privileged to serve as pastor of Presbyterian churches in Períco, Varadero, Versalles, and San José de los Ramos.

## Encounter with a Passionate Teacher

I met him in Cuba. It was the 1960s. He was a simple man, serene and reflective. His name? C. I. Itty.

Who was C. I. Itty? He was a member of the Syrian Orthodox Church and a citizen of India. How did he influence my life? Is it possible that a lay Orthodox theologian from India would make a decisive contribution to forming the ecumenical commitment of an ordained Presbyterian woman from Cuba? Yes! And this is precisely the "miracle" or "the miracles" that occur daily in ecumenical circles.

C. I. Itty visited Cuba while he was working with the laity program of the World Council of Churches. For him, "teaching the poor," was fundamental and something he had always done. C. I. Itty began his ministry in the 1950s, teaching in poor communities in India and Indonesia through the Christian student movement. Human relationships always took priority over any institutional or structural obligations for him. For that reason, he approached me in the midst of a large gathering organized by the Ecumenical Council of Cuba. The directness of his question surprised me: "What are your plans for the future?" I told him that I was preparing to study for a Masters in Christian Education in Great Britain. He nodded his head in a gesture characteristic of Indian persons. "You must go to Bossey, to the Ecumenical Institute in Bossey, Switzerland. You need to strengthen your vision of ecumenism so that you can help Cuba's ecumenical movement." I was not convinced. Why get more involved in the ecumenical movement? Why learn more about ecumenism? What was this all about?

We then went together to the Presbyterian church's summer camp for a spiritual retreat. And there, in the chapel (an open-air chapel, surrounded by the beauty of the Cuban countryside with its huts and royal palm trees), Itty spoke to us. He asked us to look around at the fields and at the peasants who were working nearby. Then he said, "The church must be like this chapel—

with doors wide open to see what is all around it, to never lose the perspective of those who live and work near to us." A church without walls! A wide open church! This was ecumenism!

This understanding of the ecumenical movement came from C. I. Itty's own experience; from something he called "signs and conversion":

- A new conversion to the world, a new engagement with social problems and their demand for social change
- A conversion to mission, to present the gospel message to those who are not Christians
- A new rhythm of life, worship and work, contemplation and action, distance and commitment, social service and social action, suffering and rejoicing, doubt and hope, repentance and pardon
- New understanding of the cosmic vision of redemption, the worldwide nature of Christianity, the sacramental character of the church, and the sacramental vision of life and work

## Ecumenical Vision in Formation

After the encounter with C. I. Itty, I was totally convinced, and in 1967 my church sent me to the "Ecumenical Institute of Bossey." This signified a radical change in my life and in the direction of my ministry. I studied for five months in the graduate school at Bossey and then spent three months visiting lay academies through Europe in the first CLLT program of the World Council of Churches (lay training course for eighteen persons from around the world). As the finale of this learning experience, my church sent me as a delegate to the Assembly of the World Council of Churches in Uppsala, Sweden (1968).

My ecumenical vision has broadened so much that I decided that this year of ecumenical encounters would not be complete without a visit to the Vatican, so I organized a visit for my Bossey roommate and myself. We were officially received by Dr. Thomas Stransky and the Pontifical Commission for Christian Unity. This visit by "only two students of Bossey" led to annual visits by all the students in Bossey's graduate school by special Vatican invitation.

## Vocation to Create a Home

I returned to Cuba with a lifelong commitment to the ecumenical movement. Upon arriving, I became the director of the Center for Studies of the Ecumenical Council of Cuba (1969). There I worked with the council's member denominations to design an ecumenical curriculum for Sunday schools that was subsequently used for ten years.

The wide open church! The church without walls! For me, these were and still are both a living reality and a permanent call.[4]

I married a Baptist pastor, Rev. Daniel Montoya, in 1970. By mutual agreement he became Presbyterian because the Baptist Convention in the eastern part of the island where he lived would not have accepted my pastoral vocation.

From the beginning we insisted that we each serve in local churches. I believe we were the first clergy couple, each serving a local church and receiving the corresponding salaries. One of the most beautiful experiences of my life was administering the sacraments during the early months of my pregnancy with my only daughter. I was sure that God was blessing these sacramental acts in a special way precisely because I carried within me the gift of new life.

## Vision and Reconstruction of the Biblical Revelation

Women's spirituality is seriously damaged when the biblical revelation is distorted. Distortion restricts a woman's ability to utilize her own experience as a revelation of God's qualities and activities. It can actually alienate a woman from her own experience when she presumes that 'the Holy' is not at all like herself."[5]

It is true that patriarchy is not the theme of the Bible; that the Bible transcends patriarchy. But it is interesting that anthropologists, historians, and biblical scholars have exhaustively analyzed historical, cultural, literary, and even socioeconomic questions while simply taking for granted the patriarchal social structures found in the Bible.

It is a marvelous spiritual experience to "reconstruct" the true role of women by reading the underlying messages in the biblical texts. How this reconstruction of the biblical revelation helped me to reconstruct my own life! It enabled me to explore more deeply the roots of my faith, of my life as a Christian.

## Ecumenical Vocation as Engagement with the Most Vulnerable

In 1985 I was interviewed by the World Council of Churches for two positions: professor at the Ecumenical Institute at Bossey or director of the WCC Department of Education. I surprised everyone by selecting Bossey; it offered less money and power, but it meant living in community in a rural setting.

Imagine what a huge change a move to a highly developed capitalist country and also living in a city would have entailed for me and my family! Three years later, when I began work with the WCC, we continued to live in Bossey, and my daughter's education took place in a strong community environment.

Developing women leaders was the priority of the program for theological education for Latin America and the Caribbean. My commitment as director of the program was to provide support for women as theologians and for the seminaries and other organizations in the region that were working successfully with women. We decided that 100 percent of our program funds would be devoted to this purpose.

This program, together with other activities of the Decade of Churches in Solidarity with Women, bore much fruit. What a joy to look around Latin America now and see so many female colleagues whose theological education was enabled by the program I directed. In 1997 we hosted a gathering of the Community of Latin American Theological Schools at our seminary in Matanzas, Cuba. The purpose of the meeting was a dialogue with some of the "fathers" of liberation theology. I was very moved when twelve prominent women leaders, with whom I had become connected through my work at the World Council, organized a tribute to me, saying, "You were our mother of liberation theology."

## Return to Cuba

I became rector of the Evangelical Theological Seminary in 1996, although I did not move back to Cuba until April 1, 1997—my birthday and, in Switzerland, Fool's Day. Friends there laughed and jokingly called me a "fool" for returning to Cuba. I was thrilled to be back. The seminary has been the protagonist of Cuban theology. If there is a place where the theologies of liberation are present in Cuba, it is this seminary. I understand Christian faith as an affirmation of life abundant—life in both the material and the spiritual sense. Anything that destroys life negates Christian faith. Everyone deserves education, health care, and housing. Human rights are an affirmation of life. For this reason I greatly appreciate our society's success in tending to the most needy, its focus on those that are traditionally ignored.

## A New Vision for Ecumenical Learning

It is interesting that the enterprise of women gathering for theological reflection—unraveling the strands of biblical interpretation, figuring out the mysteries of theological dogma, and moving forward with projects of ecclesial and societal transformation to build a better world—has consistently been sustained by ecumenical learning. I will never forget the first gathering of Latin American women theologians in 1979 in Mexico. There were women of every descent, women of various Roman Catholic orders, and women from a wide variety of Protestant and evangelical denominations. It was an ecumenical miracle that continues to the present day.

It can not be otherwise, given our belief that "ecumenical learning occurs when diverse people, rooted in their respective faith traditions and their own complex experiences with regard to culture, gender, nationality, race, class, and so forth, open up to the richness of each other's perspectives and seek together to know God and to be faithful to the role that God has for them in the world."[6] The Sixth Assembly of the World Council of Churches, celebrated in 1983 in Vancouver, identified ecumenical learning as a priority, defining it as a process that consists of

1. Common witness, liturgy, and spiritual formation
2. Learning about the faith traditions of other churches, as well as one's own church
3. Biblical and theological literacy and preparation for ecumenical leadership

The Sixth Assembly of the WCC marked a transition to a new educational methodology which emphasized *participation in a learning community* rather than *consumption of information* presented by experts. Increasingly, the emphasis was put on being a learning community in order to become part of the household of God (1 Peter 2). I believe that this process has been especially important for women theologians and pastors.

## Ecumenical Learning Communities

As women, we are constantly forming "ecumenical communities of learning."[7] We do so to study the Bible, to develop worship services full of extraordinary collective symbols, and to seek peace with justice, gender equality, and ecological harmony. Our theological statements are poetic, in tune with life's rhythms. At the same time they express a serious ecumenical commitment to working for a church and a society where women and men are fulfilled as persons in God's image and as subjects of history.

All of these groups and gatherings have been "ecumenical" not just because the participants belong to a variety of confessions but also because, in Letty Russell's words, "they become ecumenical as they notice that the struggles of women to become fully human as God created them are wider than any confessional barrier."[8]

## Ecumenical Leadership

The principle that Dr. Carol J. Schlueter applies to feminist homiletics also applies to women's participation in ecumenical leadership. She writes,

> Feminist homiletics arise out of a community of people, a substantial number of them women, discussing the biblical material in the context of their lives. It does not arise from individuals writing sermons in isolation using solitary exegesis. Feminist homiletics recognized what I call the Canada Goose Principle. Canada geese fly in a 'V' formation and no one bird is always the leader, but each takes its turn. Upon tiring, the leader drops back and another bird replaces it. The well-being of each bird is important to the survival of the flock; and the more birds that share in the leadership, the easier it is for the flock to progress well.[9]

I believe women have made an important contribution to the understanding of how to build Christian community. It is not easy to break out of "patriarchal models," to create new models based on a completely different understanding of power and authority. For example, How does one exercise power and authority within a paradigm of participation, not domination? Our dreams and visions as women found expression in the final message of a ten-day seminar, "Women in Dialogue," celebrated in 1994, half-way through the Decade of Churches in Solidarity with Women.

> We are united
> by our solemn rejection of the pervasive, growing
>     violence against women in the whole world;
> by our hope in the freedom born of faith
>     in Mary's son, Jesus; and
> by our desire for a new, whole community of human beings,
>     earth and all creatures, within the embrace of God.[10]

## Spiritual Journey of Encounters and Visions

My journey has followed the signs of the times—ecumenical time of encounters and visions. My encounters have been inspired by faith. I have felt the power of the Spirit in all that I have done, and today I sense God's call more strongly than ever. To affirm my vocation means to confront new challenges, to be creative, to work for the well-being of both church and society. My visions have had ecumenical roots and have been sustained by God during long years of dedication as a pastor, a professor, and a theologian. The places where I have worked—the congregations, the councils, the seminary—have been a garden where, together with many friends and colleagues, I have witnessed how seeds of faith transform dreams into plans and visions into reality.

Speaking for all those who have accompanied me on this journey, I can say that we have planted seeds of freedom, dignity, and love. And now we see flowers blooming everywhere: in cities, in the countryside, in churches, in homes, in theological seminaries, and on university campuses. The flowers are of many different colors and smells. They announce that spring has arrived, and with the coming of spring, we know that dreaming is still possible.

Chapter 12

# Risky Business

## Jean Marie Peacock

*Jean Marie Peacock is associate pastor of Lakeview Presbyterian Church in New Orleans, a congregation impacted heavily by Hurricane Katrina. She has a M.Div. from Louisville Presbyterian Theological Seminary and a Masters in Social Work from Arizona State University. Jean Marie spent seven years as a PC(USA) mission worker, primarily in border ministry.*

*I*t was the year 2000, and I had recently been ordained to the ministry of the Word and Sacrament. The phone rang. "May I speak with Reverend Peacock?" asked the voice on the other end of the phone. "This is she," I responded. The person on the other end didn't immediately identify himself. He asked again, "Is Reverend Peacock there?"

"This is she. How can I help you?" I responded.

"Is your husband there?" the person asked.

"My husband is not here at the moment," I explained. "Can I help you with something?"

"Well, I need to talk to the pastor. I'll call back later to see if he is home."

"Don't hang up yet," I replied. "You are speaking to the pastor. My husband is a biologist."

There was a long pause at the other end of the phone, and then came the revelation as the caller exclaimed, "Oh, you're a *woman* pastor."

Yes, I am a woman, and I am a pastor. It is not uncommon for me to serve as a guest preacher at a church and to be greeted after the service with comments such as "This is the first time that I ever heard a woman preach, and I could hear every word you said." I am looking forward to that day when being a woman and a pastor will no longer be considered a novelty by church members and by the broader society. As we work toward that day, I give thanks to

Jean Marie Peacock answers questions shortly after her election as Vice Moderator of the General Assembly in 2004. (*Photo taken by David P. Young, courtesy of the Office of Communications, General Assembly Council, Presbyterian Church (U.S.A.).*)

God for those who have been pioneers, paving the way for women to serve as leaders in the ministry of the church.

Yes, I am a woman, and I am a pastor. God has called me, through the community of faith and by the power of the Holy Spirit, to serve Christ's church as a minister of the Word and Sacrament. I confess, however, that this call to ordained ministry has involved struggle, doubts, and questions. I never imagined myself serving the church in ordained ministry. In fact, I would characterize myself as having had an "on again, off again" relationship with the institutional church.

I grew up in the church. My father is a United Methodist minister. My parents raised my brother, sister, and me to be active in the life of the church. As a family, we prayed together, worshiped together, and lived our faith by serving others in the larger community. When I graduated from high school, I attended the College of Wooster, a college affiliated with the Presbyterian Church (U.S.A.). There, I was active in the campus ministry program. I knew that I loved Christ, and I wanted to serve him in the world.

As a young adult, I became increasingly disillusioned with the institutional church, which seemed to me to be all too willing to water down and "sell out" the gospel in the midst of society's competing values. I encountered more than one church and church-related organization where, in my opinion, sexism, racism, and materialism overshadowed the witness to Christ's way of peace and justice. Men dominated, and women and people of color were often not included in decision-making structures.

While I questioned my role in the church, Christ continued to place a strong claim on my life. I skirted around the fringe of the church, searching for a way to serve God in the world. It was from the fringe—from the margins—that God called me into ministry. There were no burning bushes, no flashes of lightening, no parting of the heavens. This call from God felt as if a force stronger than gravity had taken hold of me and was pulling me toward mission service. The call was so powerful, and God's hold on me so strong, that I knew I had no choice but to go where I was being led. I was led to the U.S./Mexican border to serve in ministry with refugees from Central America.

This was a call that I couldn't explain very well to my friends and family. I'm not sure that I even understood it myself. Why go to the border? I didn't speak Spanish. I had never been farther south than Tennessee, where my grandparents lived. I didn't know how I would support myself or where I would live. Yet I felt that I had no choice but to go. I had heard of the challenges and needs facing Central American refugees as they crossed the border into the United States. I had met refugees from Central America who had shared their stories of violence, death threats, and torture. I had been convicted by those relationships to do something in response.

I first went to South Texas to the Rio Grande Valley. I drove to the border in my little Honda Civic hatchback. I took nothing with me but a backpack, which I threw haphazardly into the car. I had no idea what to expect when I arrived. I ended up working with the Overground Railroad, which posted bond for refugees to be released from immigration detention centers in the United States and helped them apply for political asylum in Canada. I worked for the summer with a couple who took me into their home. We went to the detention center daily, where we spent hours interviewing refugees and preparing their asylum applications. Since I didn't speak Spanish, my job was to greet the refugees as they waited to be interviewed and to type up the asylum applications.

I quickly became aware that we were a very small operation in the midst of huge need. There were hundreds of refugees in the detention center. Each day we heard horrendous stories of torture and rape and massacres from people who had survived the violence. We met with people who had received death threats. We met people who had left everything behind, including children and family, as they fled for their lives. They came north, seeking safe haven from the violence and persecution. In the United States, they faced deportation back to the oppression they had fled. Canada, however, recognized their status as refugees and offered them political asylum.

We had very little time to process a refugee's request for political asylum. We had to work quickly to interview refugees and post bond to release them from detention. Our problem, however, was that we had limited resources. There were hundreds of refugees in detention. We could not help everyone. It was an agonizing experience as we tried to decide whom to help. Who had the worst stories of torture and rape? Who was most at risk of being killed if deported? We knew that our decisions could mean life or death to those we were seeking to help.

In my second week of this work, I had a nightmare that haunts me to this day. In the dream, I was standing on a bridge and there were people drowning in the river below. They were screaming frantically for help. I jumped into the water and started pulling people to the shore, but all around me people were drowning. I could not work fast enough to save everyone.

The next morning, I shared this dream with the couple with whom I was living and working. We had a long conversation about the sinfulness inherent in a situation where we must choose whom to save. "No one should be in the position in which we find ourselves," one of my colleagues said to me. "It is a sin that unjust systems have created this situation. It is a sin that oppression and violence in Central America is causing so much pain and suffering. It is a sin that immigration policies in the United States have failed to provide Central American refugees with much-needed safe haven." Then he made a comment that has remained with me all these years: "God has put you in this place, Jean Marie, not as a rescuer but as a witness to the injustice. Here, you have met Christ tortured and crucified in your neighbors. Your life will never be the same because of it."

He was right. My life has never been the same. Our lives are changed—transformed—as we meet Christ in our neighbors. Through these encounters we develop a deeper relationship with Christ himself. To be the church is to struggle to follow the One we confess as our Lord and Savior, to follow the One who fully entered into our pain and suffering, dying on the cross for our salvation. To follow Christ is to ask, "Where are crucifixions happening today? Who is being tortured or oppressed? Who is drowning or dying? Where is the suffering?" Then, we must go to these places, for wherever there is suffering, wherever there is pain, we are sure to meet Christ in that place.

That was my experience, as I followed God's call to ministry with persons struggling to survive on the margins of society. After that summer in the Rio Grande Valley, I served the Presbyterian Church (U.S.A.) for seven years as a mission volunteer and as a mission diaconate worker on the U.S./Mexican border in Tucson, Arizona, and in Mexico. I arrived in Tucson in August, 1985. At that time, several ministers, priests, and church workers were facing trial for providing "sanctuary" to undocumented Central American refugees. The sanctuary movement was a faith-based effort of churches and synagogues that provided safe haven to refugees who might otherwise be deported by immigration back to the persecution and violence they had fled in their homelands. Southside Presbyterian Church in Tucson was one of the first churches in the nation to declare itself a sanctuary for Central American refugees in March, 1982. A movement developed, as churches and synagogues across the nation made similar public declarations of sanctuary. Among them were Presbyterian churches around the country who provided refugees with transportation, housing, and other assistance throughout the 1980s and early 1990s.

Those involved in the sanctuary movement accepted the risk of being arrested, tried, and imprisoned for their efforts to protect Central American refugees from deportation. There were several cases of arrests and federal court trials throughout the sanctuary movement. Presbyterians were not immune to federal prosecution. The pastor of Southside Presbyterian Church, the Reverend John Fife, was among sixteen church workers and sixty refugees arrested and indicted on January 14, 1985, for their involvement in the sanctuary movement. Other Presbyterians included Kay Kelley and Mary Ann Lundy, who were named as unindicted coconspirators. They both refused to testify in the federal trial against their colleagues and were placed under house arrest. The General Assemblies of 1985 and 1986 expressed support for the ministry of sanctuary and for the governing bodies and individual Presbyterians involved in it.

While colleagues were in court facing trial, I became very involved in coordinating the underground railroad of the sanctuary movement. Through this involvement in sanctuary, I joined many other people of faith as we challenged inhumane applications of United States immigration law, risking court battles and imprisonment as we sought to bring the U.S. government into compliance with international laws that protect refugees who flee persecution. In this ministry, we assisted refugees with safe passage north. We also coordinated efforts nationally to provide them with housing, food, legal advice, medical attention, and transportation. We communicated frequently with human rights groups and churches in Mexico and Central America. On several occasions, I traveled to Central America to meet with human rights groups and church workers who were the targets of death squads.

On one trip to El Salvador, I visited a parish where pictures of the martyrs of the congregation lined the wall of the fellowship hall. Many had been killed by the military because they were seen as "subversives." One member of the church said to me, "If it is subversive to proclaim the gospel in the midst of violence and oppression, then I am guilty." This church held literacy classes, teaching people to read and discuss the Bible, activities that were considered subversive. The church also documented human rights violations and sought justice for the families of victims. Their involvement in these ministries often resulted in violent death.

On the Sunday that I joined this congregation in worship, soldiers stood at the doors of the church, pointing their guns into the congregation. I felt intimidated and afraid. I knew that members of the church had been killed in the past when soldiers had opened fire on the congregation during worship.

In that context, the cost of discipleship became very real to me. So too did the witness of the church in proclaiming Christ's victory over sin and death. At one point in the service, the names of those from the congregation who had been recently martyred were read aloud. As each name was read, the congregation responded in unison, *"Presente."* "Present." It was a powerful witness to the resurrection. As one member of the church explained to me later, "They may kill the body, but they cannot kill the Spirit."

My call to the ministry of Word and Sacrament has been shaped by these experiences—by the powerful witness of Christ's church to God's saving power. In that church in El Salvador, I experienced the power of Christ's resurrection as never before. My fear of death subsided, as we affirmed God's power to sustain life beyond death. *"Presente,"* we shouted. Our sisters and brothers in Christ, though they had been killed, still lived. *"Presente,"* we said, affirming that their witness to God's love lives on. *"Presente,"* we shouted, in recognition that God's Spirit is always present with us for all eternity. "What is there to fear?" my Salvadoran friend affirmed. "They may kill the body, but they will never extinguish the love of God."

In El Salvador, people of faith have literally given their lives to proclaim the gospel with integrity, to engage in ministry with the poor, to teach people how to read the Bible, and to live by God's love, peace, and justice. They have lost their lives or were imprisoned or tortured because they witnessed to God's word of hope and liberation in the midst of the oppression. Their complete dedication to living and preaching the gospel, no matter the cost, has greatly influenced my understanding of ministry as "risky business."

I entered seminary in 1995, completing my first year at Colgate Rochester Divinity School in Rochester, New York. In my application to seminary, I wrote, "My life and faith has been radically transformed by my interactions with people who are involved in liberation struggles in various parts of the world. In particular, the witness of Central Americans has taught me that faith involves persistence, courage, and hope in the struggle for justice, even in the face of death, imprisonment, and torture. They have brought me to a deeper relationship with a liberating God, whose saving power lifts us into hope and light, even in the darkest times. They have challenged me to trust more fully in God's redemptive power and to live more fully into God's love."

In December 1999, I graduated from Louisville Presbyterian Theological Seminary. As I prepared for examination for ordination, these experiences in the mission field continued to permeate my understandings of the call to ministry of Word and Sacrament. They surfaced as I wrote a confession of faith to share with the Committee on Preparation for Ministry. I asked one of my seminary professors to read it and to make comments on it. He returned it to me several days later. He had written his comments on the confession, in red ink. One comment, in particular, stands out: "Are you a candidate for ministry or a lightening rod?" In one paragraph, I had written, "I believe that God's call to love others is the supreme law by which I must live my life. I profess that my allegiance to God comes first, over and above any church denomination, government, or country. I believe that Christians must work to change civil law, political or economic structures, or church polity whenever they fail to protect justice and dignity for all people. I believe that Scripture contains a radical message that turns upside down power structures which value profit and prestige over love and service." In red ink, next to this paragraph, I found another comment: "You will, no doubt, get questions on this from presbytery."

I did face a rather intense discussion of my confession of faith when I met with the Committee on Preparation for Ministry. By the time I arrived on the floor of presbytery to be examined, I felt ready to address any question that might arise. The questions and answers went more smoothly than I had expected, and the presbytery voted unanimously to approve my ordination to the ministry of the Word and Sacrament.

I was ordained in April 2000 to serve as a redevelopment pastor at Berry Boulevard Presbyterian Church in Louisville, Kentucky. I had served that congregation in my last year as a student in seminary. In the context of church transformation/redevelopment, ministry as "risky business" took on new meaning. God often calls us out into the world, beyond our comfort zones, to share the good news of the gospel with others. As the congregation and I sought new ways to reach out to the surrounding neighborhood, we started to knock on the doors of homes in the community to introduce ourselves. This became an experience of spiritual renewal, as we heard God calling us beyond the walls of the church into the community. We began to organize worship services outdoors, in a nearby park, where we invited people playing and picnicking in the park to worship with us. We also explored ways that the church could become more inviting to outsiders. This was challenging ministry, filled with newness and change that led us into unknown territory.

In the midst of this new experience of ministry, I learned from my husband that he had received an exciting job offer in New Orleans. We have two very different careers in our marriage—that of a research biologist and a pastor. In this instance, we decided to make the move with his career. Soon after our arrival in New Orleans, I was called to serve as the Associate Pastor at Lakeview Presbyterian Church.

To be a minister of Word and Sacrament is to be called by God, through the community of faith, to proclaim the good news of God's saving power in the midst of sin and death. What I continue to discover in my ministry is that this is no easy task. It is a challenge to proclaim the gospel with integrity and to facilitate the sacramental life of a congregation, such that God's people are drawn into a deeper relationship with Christ as Savior and engage their faith more fully in the world. This challenge often requires more than I feel I am able to give. I bring to ministry all my weaknesses, doubts, and apprehensions. Sometimes I feel like a hypocrite, wondering how I can preach the gospel with integrity, given my own failure to follow Christ as fully and as faithfully as God desires.

"Give up everything and follow me." "The last shall be first, and the first shall be last." "Turn the other cheek." "Love your enemies; do good to those who hate you." "Love your neighbor as yourself." "What you did unto the least of these, you did unto me" "Take up your cross and follow me." These are hard teachings of Christ. They are not necessarily difficult to understand, but they are difficult to live fully and faithfully, given the pressures and values of today's world. To proclaim God's Word and to administer the sacraments such that God's people are drawn more deeply into a relationship with Christ as Savior, is countercultural, because Christ's way is so different from the messages of power, prestige, and consumerism that flood our society and our lives. The temptation is always present to sugarcoat Christ's teachings, to make Jesus more palatable, to ease our discomfort at what he is really asking of us, to water down the faith to our liking.

The only way that I can begin to proclaim the gospel with any sense of integrity is by confessing my own complicity in sin, my own need for God's saving grace. There are many times when courage fails me, when the risks seem too great, when I falter and fail to speak the truth in love. I recognize the challenge of proclaiming the gospel in the context of wealth, comfort, and privilege that dominates so much of American society, because I recognize my own complicity in structures that perpetuate the unjust distribution of resources at a cost to so many in the world.

When God called me to the ministry of Word and Sacrament, I heard that call in the form of a question—a question I shared in my application to seminary:

"How do we build experiences of Christian community in our congregations where we challenge each other to radically live Christ's teachings in the context of today's world?" Inherent in that question is my understanding that all of us need the support of the community of faith to sustain us in the ministry and mission to which God calls us. Ministry is the work of all God's people. I believe that an important role of clergy is to facilitate the mission of the church by empowering people to be ministers to each other and to our world.

Jesus calls us to follow him—to go with him into the places of pain and suffering in our world—to heal the sick, feed the hungry, clothe the naked, visit the imprisoned, and walk the paths of peace and justice. It is a ministry of all God's people. "How do we build experiences of Christian community in our congregations where we challenge each other to radically live Christ's teachings in the context of today's world?" The question still challenges me in my ministry, as God has now called me to serve not only as an associate pastor of a congregation in New Orleans but as the Vice Moderator of the 216th General Assembly of the Presbyterian Church (U.S.A.).

# Chapter 13

# Outsiders Within: Women in Ministry

## Letty M. Russell

*Letty M. Russell, Professor Emerita of Theology, Yale Divinity School, was ordained to the ministry in 1958. Pastor for seventeen years and teacher of theology for thirty-two years, she is an author, ecumenical leader, and feminist. Her theology is concerned with all forms of human liberation.*

*I* join this one-hundred-year celebration of Presbyterian women in ordained ministry with a life full of memories related to the fifty years of women's ordination to the Word and Sacrament. I was ordained as a pastor in 1958, serving seventeen years in the East Harlem Protestant Parish in New York City, and then thirty-two years as a teacher of theology at Manhattan College and Yale Divinity School. My years of full-time ministry stretch across this fifty-year period that we celebrate, but these years are not all about celebration. They reflect a "love/hate relationship" with a denomination that has often viewed me as an *outsider within.*[1]

I have found myself serving within the structures of the Presbyterian Church and of ecumenical and academic institutions yet always knowing that there is something that makes me a "square peg in a round hole." My woman's body and woman's way of work somehow does not measure up to the father stereotype of a Protestant pastor. Even today with ever-increasing numbers of talented and gracious women in church leadership, the question of where they fit into the male-dominated hierarchy of the church is ever with us. This question about the changing role of women continues to be debated among conservative churches and members of our congregations who would like to turn back the clock in an effort to reach "blessed assurance" that their world does not need to change.

In the midst of social structures designed to push out, or down, anyone who does not fit the right model because of race, class, nationality, gender, or sexual orientation, I have discovered many networks of wonderful people devoted to the work of justice and partnership. Over the years many changes have happened in the church in the United States and abroad, and one of them is the increasing contribution of outsiders to what has been a white, Eurocentric, male church structure. This I celebrate as I reflect on my own journey as a woman who is *in but still out* of the church, and how that has led me to view our call to ministry in a *church inside out*. My experience as an outsider within has also led me to embrace a ministry of *solidarity with strangers*.

## In But Still Out

In 1973 Elizabeth Howell Verdesi published a book on the history of women's work in the Presbyterian Church entitled *In But Still Out: Women in the Church*.[2] She documented two events in which women in the church lost their access to power and decision making in the denomination. In the 1920s the Women's Board of Missions found itself restructured into the boards and agencies of the church so that it no longer controlled its finances or the work of women in mission. Again in the 1940s and 1950s women had a potential power base in Christian education and allowed it to be co-opted by the larger structures of the church.

We know that there are many reasons for such events, but we also know that the experience of women in the church has sometimes been one of diminishment and restructuring if not downright hostility. The General Assemblies are frequently the scene of ever-new strategies to contain efforts that would empower young women and reach out in new ways to the coming generations. This sort of political action by those competing to control church structures affects the role of lay women as well as those who are ordained deacons, elders, and ministers of Word and Sacrament. In fact, becoming an outsider within is a common experience for groups of persons who "miss the mark" because they are not white, Euro-american, affluent, heterosexual, able-bodied, or male.

## Making Sense of Ministry

Making sense of what ministry means for women and men within structures of oppression or marginality due to racism, sexism, and classism has been one of my lifelong concerns. In fact, it has been my concern for so long that the list keeps growing—with imperialism, ableism, heterosexism, globalization, environmental destruction, and more! Nor have I been able to ignore the fact that as an educated, white, Euro-american woman I benefit from many of the privileges that come from such social sins. Yet I am always status inconsistent: a woman who has authority in the church as a pastor and theologian but also a bisexual feminist who advocates for the full humanity of *all* women, together with *all* men in harmony with the creation.

I came by my "misfit-ness" at an early age. In kindergarten I ran away from Sunday school and crossed all the forbidden streets to tell my mother that there was nothing there to interest a girl like me! By 7th grade I was already 5'8" and the tallest girl in the class, a "tomboy" who did not fit! When I followed my mother's footsteps and went to Wellesley College, I thought I would really fit. But I had not counted on the fact that I lived in a co-op dorm where all the daughters of ministers and missionaries and less affluent families were collected. I compounded this difference by electing to major in religion, a universally disliked subject because it was required in the sophomore year. One day on the train to New York I told my businessman father that I was going to work in the church as a Christian educator. He said, "You will be sorry because *you will always be a misfit*!"

In 1951 I went to work in the East Harlem Protestant Parish in New York City and found myself as an outsider who was welcomed within! There I was accepted even though I did not fit in a poor, Puerto Rican and black ghetto. After three years in East Harlem I recognized the need for ordination in order to work in the power structure of the church. I applied to Harvard Divinity School although they did not admit women, saying that it was time that they did. To my surprise, I was accepted and became one of the first two women to complete three years and graduate from this school.

The United Presbyterian Church U.S.A. didn't ordain women, and it had no jobs for women pastors. However, many other women and men had caught the Spirit of reform, and by the time I graduated, I was able to become the first woman ordained in my presbytery and to return to East Harlem as a pastor. There I was lucky. In spite of my connections to power through whiteness, education, and now ordination, I continued to be accepted as "just Letty."

After seventeen years in East Harlem I finished my Th.D. at Union Theological Seminary, married Hans Hoekendijk, and went to teach at the Christian Brother's Manhattan College in the Bronx. When I was interviewed at what was then a men's college, the Brother who was President was disappointed because I was not African American and only represented two outsider slots: woman and Protestant. He said to me, "What are you anyway?" I answered him, "I am a Father, Brother!" They must have been hard up because I got the job.

Letty M. Russell greets the youth group at the Presbyterian Church of the Ascension in New York City soon after her ordination. (*Courtesy of the author.*)

## Becoming a Feminist

For me, there has been no separation between my religious faith and the feminist movement. Those of us who struggle for empowerment in church institutions are simply part of the larger and very diverse movement for inclusion and empowerment of women in all fields and all parts of the world. The movement has helped to make sense of what is a common experience for many outsiders and oppressed groups because it names the contradictions in our lives so that we can see them and work with others to change them.

Feminism came into my life while I was in East Harlem engaged in the struggles of the civil rights movement. When I read Betty Friedan and Mary Daly in the late 1960s I knew right away that they were describing another structure of oppression. This one included me in the oppressed group as well as in the oppressor group. I began writing women's liberation material for the church and the National Board of the YWCA in the early 1970s and joined other women in the ecumenical movement, creating an international women's network through the World Council of Churches. Writing *Human Liberation in a Feminist Perspective: A Theology*[3] helped me make sense of my experience in justice work and my experience as a woman. It was also the title of a course I was teaching at Yale in 1974. I tried to show that liberation theology, black theology and feminist theology have the same liberating roots in the Christian tradition and that "no one is free until all are free."

The book grew out of a network of resistance and struggle in the World Council of Churches (WCC), for whom I was involved in a study on "Christians in Changing Institutions." I could not get them to include a feminist group in the study, so I created one in New York City and met with women at Union Theological Seminary and at the Interchurch Center to decide how Christian women *were* changing institutions! I wrote a report. Always needing reports, the WCC published it under the title "Human Liberation in a Feminine Perspective." It began a network, "WOW: Women of the World," that continued working to change the WCC. Our campaign to increase the participation of women in the WCC resulted in a decision to mandate 25 percent women delegates at the 1975 Assembly in Nairobi rather than the existing 2 percent. Afterwards we changed our name to RSAC (Ad Hoc Group on Racism, Sexism, and Classism), and we have kept on going ever since! Thirty years later we have added *ageism* to our title!

## Gift of Not Fitting

Through the feminist movement I discovered that being a misfit is a gift and opportunity for *a revolution of small changes*.[4] It allows us to understand the meaning of hospitality and honoring difference from the side of the stranger. When I speak of God's welcoming of the stranger and our partnership in this welcoming action for all religions, races, and genders, I can do so, at least in part, as one who claims what postcolonial feminists call *hybridity*. I am *both outside and within* institutional power structures. As an advocate of peace with justice I can work together with others for the empowerment of all peoples, "regardless."

This practice of God's hospitality means that I am constantly looking for ways to empower other outsiders in the institutions where I work and live. I always have to ask myself as I gather with a group, "Who is missing? Who are the ones whose voice is not heard?" As a Christian I learned this perspective from the gospel message of Jesus Christ. I have also found that it makes sense of the rhetoric of the feminist movement. For instance, in 1988 I joined Mercy Oduyoue, Ada Maria Isasi-Diaz, and Kwok Pui-lan in editing a book entitled *Inheriting our Mothers' Gardens*.[5] In inviting women to tell the stories of their mothers we were encouraging women to find their own identity and self-worth and to honor their own way of thinking theologically. At the same time it provided an opening for women writers of color to be published so that they would have an easier time trying to break into publishing and become outsiders within.

I value being an outsider within because it keeps me on edge looking for the *power quotient* in any situation and struggling for change. In fact, I worried about going to teach at Yale in 1972 because my own racial and class background fit too well. But I need not have worried! A woman teaching feminist, queer, and liberation theologies is not quite up to that old norm. Here I was "a triangular peg in a round hole." The faculty always wondered how I managed to get in, and I always was determined to make the most of it!

I learned in East Harlem and ever since that in God's sight no one is a misfit, and I thank God for the second women's movement[6] and the opportunity to be part of making sense of women's lives. Even in my retirement I continue to be an outsider within because Yale managed to make me *a misfit forever*. They gave me a certificate of retirement that described me in male terms. Unable to write Latin or to think that a woman might have been around long enough to retire, they wrote on my certificate, "*emeritus* professor of theology"! When last heard from they had not figured out how to change my title to *emerita*. At least the church has simply allowed me to be honorably retired.

## Church Inside Out

In 1966 my late husband, Hans Hoekendijk, published a book entitled *The Church Inside Out*.[7] The perspective of this collection of essays on God's mission and the church was that God is at work in the world to mend the creation. The church does not have a mission. It is invited to be part of God's mission and to witness to God's love in the world. This perspective helps to make sense of what ministry is all about. The ministry is not ours. Nor does it belong to the church. Rather the ministry of service to humankind is the ministry of

God in Christ reconciling the world. The church is invited to participate in that ministry. Yet in many churches the minister is the one who is supposed to take care of the flock, rather than equipping the saints for their service in the world. One question that has puzzled me over the years is why the church is so much preoccupied with what is *inside,* forgetting God's concern for justice or putting things right in the world.

## In, But Not Of the World

Paul's call in 1 Corinthians 7:29–31 is for Christians to be "in, but not of, the world," but this call is frequently ignored in our congregations. We tend to ignore issues of social sin and focus on personal morality while reducing spirituality to a search for salvation. In his letter Paul is reminding the Corinthians that they are to continue to *participate* in the ongoing life of their communities, but they are to live as if the New Creation were already at hand.[8] In contrast, many churches of our day live *of, but not in, the world*. They are "of the world" because their lives, structures, class divisions, sexual orientation, and prejudices all reflect the culture of which they are a part. They are "not in the world," however, because they refuse the task of witnessing to God's intention for New Creation by practicing works of justice and peace in the world. In order to be a church inside out, we need to open our lives to God by practicing a wholistic spirituality of connection to God, to our own bodies and ourselves, and to our neighbors in need, be they next door or on the other side of the world. Participating in the already/not yet of God's New Creation leads to bold initiatives to bring peace and justice to the world.

In my ministry as a theologian and teacher I have tried to find ways that the church can be more open to the needs of the whole world. Some of these ideas are in my book *Church in the Round: A Feminist Interpretation of the Church.* In it I describe "the church as a community of Christ, bought with a price, where everyone is welcome. It is *a community of Christ* because Christ's presence, through the power of the Spirit, constitutes people as a community gathered in Christ's name (Matt. 18:20; 1 Cor. 12:4–6). This community is *bought with a price* because the struggle of Jesus to overcome the structures of sin and death constitutes both the source of new life in the community and its own mandate to continue the same struggle for life on behalf of others (1 Cor. 6:20; Phil. 2:1–11). It is a community *where everyone is welcome* because it gathers around the table of God's hospitality. Its welcome table is a sign of the coming feast of God's mended creation, with the guest list derived from the announcements of the Jubilee year in ancient Israel (Luke 14:12–14)."[9]

## Ministry in the Round

Ministry in such a church would be a roundtable ministry that seeks to be open to those at the margins of church and society. Such a ministry would work to include those who have historically been excluded from the leadership of the church because of their race, gender, or sexual orientation. During my own ministry I have often been included in ecumenical discussions of these questions of exclusion in regard to ordination. In most of these discussions, such as those in the World Council of Churches Faith and Order Commission, the focus was on the limits of ordination, the boundaries that churches have set concerning who is qualified or disqualified for a ministry of the Word and Sacrament.

In 1979 I attended a Consultation of Faith and Order in Strasbourg, France, concerning the ordination of women. I had been in many such meetings concerning the problem of women's ordination. As far as I was concerned there was no problem with women in ministry, for I had been serving as a minister for over twenty years. But this was the first meeting in which the gathered theologians and church officials were willing to recognize that it was ordination that was the problem and not women! The problem was the church's reluctance to change their traditions to include women. Their interpretations of ministry were doctrinally sound according to their church traditions, but the understanding of ministry as Christ's continuing ministry of service has been lost in the discussion of doctrinal and structural boundaries. The admission that ordination was the problem, and not women, was such a shift that I kept writing about it afterwards as the *Strasbourg Shift*.[10] In my view we need to shift from asking, "Why should women or queer people be ordained?" to "Why should anyone be ordained as long as the structures divide lay and clergy persons and set up a hierarchy in the church?"

## One Call, Many Ministries

For a church in the round that seeks to be partners with those at the margins of church and society, ministry is an expression of Jesus Christ's continuing service in the world. Rather than protecting Christ's ministry by restricting it to church hierarchies and separating it from the needs of the world, it welcomes the possibility that all may freely serve. Christians share in the ministry of Jesus, who came not to be served, but to serve [Matt. 20:25–28]. The ways we participate in that ministry are varied and change from time to time, but we are all baptized into that ministry and continue to serve God and neighbor our entire lifetimes.

Baptism is the basic ordination for all Christians, and ordination as deacon, elder, or minister of the Word and Sacrament is the way that particular communities recognize the gifts in persons who can help to equip them for ministry. In the Presbyterian Church a person's call to pastoral ministry is discerned by asking whether they have experienced an internal call by the Holy Spirit to this form of service; whether they have the gifts, education, and experience that prepares them for a particular form of ministry; and whether the church community has need of these gifts and ways to sustain that ministry. This discernment process happens repeatedly in our lives, and our ministries change in response to the needs of the church and world. With the many shifts in the ways we are called to serve, the *Strasbourg Shift* alerts us to a need to reexamine whether particular ministries require ordination for life.

What *is* for life is the sacrament of baptism, which is a sign of God's call in our lives. Whether this service is in the church or not; whether it is paid or not; whether it is clerical or not, a particular ministry is one of many ways of living out the one calling of God in Jesus Christ. In my own life I have been in many different ministries, and I intend to continue seeking out new needs and ways of service in response to my call. This is why I like to talk about my *rewirement* rather than *retirement.* There is no way that I or any other Christian can retire from our many ministries of service.

## Solidarity with Strangers

My experience as an outsider within has clearly led me to question the rigid clergy line that divides our church communities and increases hierarchy and competition for power in our denomination. At the same time it has led me to focus on a theology of hospitality that emphasizes the calling of the church as a witness to God's intention to mend the creation by bringing about a world of justice, peace, and integrity of the natural world. There are a lot of "missing persons" in our world today whose situation of poverty, injustice, and suffering makes God weep. These missing persons are not strangers to God, for God already has reached out to care for them. They are strangers in the world who need to know that God cares through the witness of a church that practices a ministry of hospitality and justice on their behalf.

### Ministry of Hospitality

Often hospitality seems to us to be what the women of the church offer after the worship service on Sunday. We do not even stop to think of it as a form of ministry but rather assume its connotation of "tea and crumpets" or, in other contexts, of sexual services offered by "ladies of the night." Although hospitality is a form of Christian spirituality that is a basic ingredient in the biblical message, it has fallen into disuse in our churches and society.[11] Yet the biblical witness is clear. The unexpected presence of God and Christ in and through actions of hospitality are seen when Abraham and Sarah welcome divine messengers at the Oaks of Mamre and when the risen Christ is recognized in the breaking of bread in Emmaus (Gen. 18:1–15; Luke 24:13–35). Hebrews 13:2 reminds us, "Do not neglect to show hospitality to strangers, for by doing that some have entertained angels without knowing it." The many injunctions to practice hospitality to the widow, the orphan, and the stranger in thanksgiving for Israel's deliverance from bondage and for God's gifts remind us that we have been strangers welcomed by God and we are called to welcome others in return (Exod. 23:9). This practice of hospitality is the ministry of all the members of a congregation and not just church women's groups, welcoming committees, or clergy.

In Matthew 25:31–46 Jesus promises to be with those who offer hospitality to the least of our brothers and sisters. It would seem that hospitality could well be understood as *solidarity with strangers*, a mutual relationship of care and trust in which we share in the struggle for empowerment, dignity, and fullness of life.

The word for hospitality in the Greek New Testament is *philoxenia*, love of the stranger. Its opposite is *xenophobia*, hatred of the stranger.[12] The ministry of the church is to be partners with strangers, to welcome those whom Christ welcomed and thus learn to be a community in which people are made one in Jesus Christ in spite of their different classes, religious backgrounds, genders, races, and ethnic groups. Our *koinonia,* or partnership in Christ, is a gift of our baptism and not a result of being of one class, race, or sexual orientation. It is a gift that transcends real differences through participation in the mission of the church on behalf of healing the brokenness of the world, beginning with ourselves.

## Dealing with Difference

Hospitality is a two-way street of mutual ministry where we often exchange roles and learn the most from those whom we considered different or "other."[13] This has been true for me in my solidarity with women in the Circle of Concerned African Women Theologians. Four years ago some of us at Yale Divinity School and the Yale Center for Interdisciplinary Research on AIDS formed a partnership with the Circle women to work with them on their research, projects, and publications related to "Sex, Stigma and HIV/AIDS: African Women Theologians Challenging Religion, Culture and Social Practices." Two particular projects we have worked on together are publications of the Circle writings in the United States and the establishment of postdoc-toral fellowships to study at Yale and create projects that will help change the attitudes of churches toward issues of care and prevention for persons living with HIV/AIDS.[14] Sharing with the women as they claim their own power to name both the problems and solutions to the difficulties they face has chal-lenged me to be both a learner and a teacher in the struggle to face what has become a world pandemic of AIDS.

In our fractured world and church the problems of difference are never absent. We live in a world in the process of economic globalization that con-stantly forces people to migrate from one place to another to escape war, poverty, sickness, genocide, and more. We are often strangers to one another and fear the strangers in our midst and around the world. The problem that we confront is not that we are different but that we often fear difference and reject those we perceive to be outside our church, our community, our nation. This fear of difference is sometimes used by those in power as an excuse to oppress those who are of a different nationality, race, gender, sexual orientation, abil-ity, and so forth. Often churches reinforce this fear and rejection by becom-ing "safe havens" from difference, admitting only certain groups and using theological teachings to exclude those who don't fit.

From my perspective, the church needs to respond to this crisis of division by practicing a ministry of hospitality. Justice-infused hospitality can reach out across our differences and become a catalyst for partnership and commu-nity. Standing in solidarity with strangers by working against oppressive structures that make them outsiders within their own societies may help us to discover God's hospitality in our own communities as we pray for the renewal of the church as an instrument of justice and peace in the world.

I continue to understand my ministry in the Presbyterian Church (U.S.A.) from the perspective of an *outsider within*. I am glad to be in this position, how-ever, because it forces me continually to challenge the church to be a *church inside out* and to challenge myself to practice a ministry of just hospitality. When I was ordained in East Harlem in 1958 it was because I knew that I needed to be ordained in order to be able to integrate the worship life of the church with its educational ministry and justice advocacy. When I left East Harlem after sev-enteen years to begin my teaching ministry I continued to be ordained because I was simply *rewiring* and changing the location of my ministry.

Although I think that the structures of lifelong ordination should be reformed, I also believe that, as long as this process is the avenue to church leadership, all baptized Christians should be welcome to offer their gifts within and beyond the structures of the church. In particular I have continued to be ordained because it allowed me to be a model for women who are denied access to a ministry of the Word and Sacrament in other denominations, as well as a continual reminder to my own denomination that sexual orientation is no barrier to the exercise of the gifts of the Holy Spirit. In spite of all the mixed messages of hierarchy and privilege that go with ordination, the practice of ministry has been a blessing in my life, and I give thanks for the continuing experience of God's call.

Chapter 14

# Thanks Be to God!

## A Conclusion by Susan R. Andrews

*Susan R. Andrews has been a parish pastor for thirty years and a lover of the church her whole life. The daughter, granddaughter, wife, and daughter-in-law of pastors, she finds the art of ministry both a challenge and a delight. Pastor of Bradley Hills Presbyterian Church (Bethesda, Maryland), she served as moderator of the 215th General Assembly.*

*I*t was my first Sunday in my first parish. I was the new assistant pastor, the fifth of five on the pastoral staff, and the first woman pastor to serve the First Presbyterian Church in Allentown, Pennsylvania. In 1956, when Margaret Towner had been ordained as the first clergywoman in the UPCUSA, she was serving the Allentown church. But because she had originally been called as director of Christian education, she returned to that position after her ordination—and was never asked to preach or celebrate the sacraments in the Allentown church. I was humbled to be the one who, nineteen years later, exercised the privilege that should have been hers.

That first Sunday we were all a bit nervous. I led the liturgy and offered the children's sermon, a comfortable way for all of us to adjust to this new thing that God was doing. After the service, one of the fathers asked his five-year-old son, "So, how did you like the new minister?" To which the little boy answered, "Oh. That wasn't a minister. That was just a lady in a black robe."

Twenty-five years later, when I was welcoming a new associate pastor to the congregation I serve in Bethesda, Maryland, I asked him to lead the liturgy and offer the children's sermon. After the service one of our fathers asked his five-year-old daughter, "So, how did you like the new minister?" To which the little girl responded, "I didn't know that men could be ministers!"

As they say, "We've come a long way, baby!"

The powerful stories in this book joyfully proclaim that the Holy Spirit has been eagerly at work in the lives of Presbyterian women during the last one hundred years and that the entry of women into the offices of deacon, elder and minister of Word and Sacrament has been very good for the church. Each testimony witnesses to the generous grace of God that has empowered us and protected us, pushed us and changed us, softened us and strengthened us for faithful service in Christ's name. And each story begins with the extravagant waters of baptism that have nourished us in our lifelong love affair with Jesus and with his sinful, soulful church.

## A Presbyterian Story

Mine is a garden-variety, 1950s Presbyterian story. My father was a minister, and my mother was a very gifted—and very frustrated—minister's wife. Going to church was like brushing my teeth—only more fun. I loved worship. I loved the Cherub Choir. I loved vacation Bible school. I loved the organ and the velvet lining of the offering plate and the sunlight dancing on the sanctuary walls. And I was never bored. But it never occurred to me to think about being a minister when I grew up. I was going to be a mommy—and maybe a ballet dancer.

It was an odd-looking Lutheran, my college chaplain, who called me into ministry. And he had to convince me that being a pastor was something that women could do. Eventually, it was my curious mind that propelled me into seminary. But it was my humbled heart that led me into parish ministry—a heart strangely warmed by the energy and the questions and the anxieties of a bunch of junior highs, who were my field-education flock one year. And so on September 27, 1974, at the tender age of twenty-five, I was ordained into the ministry of Word and Sacrament at the Church of the Covenant in Boston—the first clergywoman ordained in Boston Presbytery, and, roughly, the 200th clergywoman ordained in the UPCUSA. How astounding—and wonderful—that in 2005 there are over four thousand of us!

Did I have any doubts that ministry was right for me? I had all kinds of doubts—and anxieties and concerns and fears. And I still do. Even after thirty years of parish ministry, after a year serving as Moderator of the 215th General Assembly, after dozens of opportunities to teach and preach across the country—after all this experience, I still can't sleep on Saturday night. I still tremble when I step into the pulpit. And I still wonder why anyone would want to listen to me—or to my feeble faith. But through it all, God has encouraged me to hold in my heart the gift of gospel, and share it with honesty and hope. And I still wake up most mornings cherishing the precious gift of my call. I can say today, without a shadow of a doubt, that God calls women just

Moderator Susan R. Andrews calling believers to remember their baptism at the 2004 General Assembly in Richmond, Virginia. (*Photo taken by David P. Young, courtesy of the Office of Communications, General Assembly Council, Presbyterian Church (U.S.A.).*)

as graciously as God calls men—because God needs all of us to create a "kin-dom" of kindness and justice and hope here on earth.

Telling the saga of women's leadership in the church has created a rich legacy of spiritual truth—each story connected to the megastory of the moth-ers and the sisters who have gone before. But it is also clear that Paul's vision of male/female equality within the church became reality because a few strong men believed in it. My own story is full of men who affirmed my call to ministry—a father who in 1974 had a special ordination certificate espe-cially printed so that the "he" would become a "she," and who took one of his own preaching robes and tailored it to female size for my ordination day; a women's college chaplain who was responsible for calling fifteen women into ministry in the 1960s and 1970s; a husband who has been my partner in love and ministry for thirty years, co-parenting and co-pastoring, and then leaving his own satisfying job in order to follow me when the Spirit called me to Bethesda; denominational staff and laymen and colleagues in parish ministry who have affirmed me and encouraged me and nurtured me into national lead-ership within the church. Let it be known that women in ministry have been richly blessed by some remarkable brothers in the faith. And those same broth-ers have been blessed in return, enriched by the dynamic energy of male/female partnerships in ministry. Yet in significant ways men and women bring different and distinctive gifts to the leadership of the church.

## A Rich Heritage

Feminist theology has had an internal tug-of-war during the past fifty years concerning the uniqueness of women's experience and leadership within the community of God's people. Do women do ministry differently? Is there a unique female "style" of leadership? Are women and men wired so differently that staff conflicts around gender issues are inevitable? Each of us will answer these questions differently. But my own experience suggests that because of culture, because of the sin of sexism, and because of inherent developmental differences, women in the last century have brought a distinctive witness within the church and within the larger world. And our script for ministry has come from some powerful matriarchs and sisters in Scripture.

When I am asked to offer a charge in an ordination service for a woman, or speak at a woman's conference, or write a letter of appreciation for a woman's service within the church, I turn to the women of Scripture as my text. Because I know that in my life and ministry it is these soft, strident, risky, risqué voices that both comfort and afflict me in my still-unfolding journey.

Eve's rebellious curiosity, Sarah's preposterous generativity, Puah's daring disobedience, Shiprah's subversive soul, Ruth's fierce faithfulness, Deborah's role-shattering partnership, Esther's brave beauty, Rebekah's conniving courage, Mary's pondering power, Magdalene's relational heart, Martha's cantankerous competence, her sister's quiet contemplation, Tabitha's joyful service, Priscilla's organizational skill. Of course, the pivotal point in the gospel narrative revolves around those early morning witnesses to the resurrection—women whose "idle tale" turned out to be God's most powerful Word of Life. As biblical Christians, we Presbyterians are shaped by the pull and power of Scripture. And within the Presbyterian Church (U.S.A.) we women have taken our marching orders from the biblical women so elegantly and eloquently created in the image of God.

One of the joys of my moderatorial year was meeting with clergywomen in small gatherings across the church. It was a way that we could celebrate the almost fifty years of grace that has shaped us for pastoral leadership within the church. And it was a way to share our joys and our sorrows as the church continues to struggle with the full acceptance of our gifts. These gatherings were markedly different than the other small groups who greeted me in presbyteries and congregations during the year.

In western Pennsylvania, clergywomen gathered from five presbyteries and were delighted to find each other in a part of the country where clergywomen are few and far between and where isolation is one of the crippling dynamics of ministry. That group was the most theologically diverse group of clergywomen I met all year. But our differences simply didn't matter. There was joy and love and acceptance in that room, an affirmation of the importance of theological differences. And a clear sense that women can model a new way of disagreeing that leads to community instead of conflict.

In western Colorado, the women decided to have a tea party! And so there we sat, busy Presbyterian feminists, drinking tea out of fine china cups, nibbling on delicate pastries, and admiring the hats that some were playfully wearing. That was an afternoon of much laughter and many tears as we shared our joys with each other, our deep satisfaction in our common calling, and the pain and anger of discrimination that many still feel in their vocational journeys. That group modeled an egalitarian sense of collegiality that was apparent across the church. Clergywomen were all mixed up with Christian educators and lay pastors. And status and role simply melted away in our conversations about Christ and the church.

And so it went, in Indianapolis, in Washington DC, in southern Ohio, in Cincinnati, in South Africa, in Detroit, in Texas—even in Ethiopia, where the women were really six hundred girls, students in a Presbyterian mission school, eager to learn in a country where 50 percent of females are illiterate. Those gatherings of women, combined with my observations of the ministries carried out by lay and ordained women across the church, have led me to some tentative thoughts about the distinctiveness of women's leadership in the church. And the essays in this book simply reinforce my thinking. There are at least two dynamics of female leadership that are changing the way we do church.

## Incarnational Leadership

Marcus Borg has suggested that there are three macrostories in Scripture—that of exodus, exile, and resurrection.[1] And each one of them provides a metaphorical script for faithful living, a way of understanding both the gift and the cost of being God's person in the world. Traditional Christian doctrine emphasizes the resurrection narrative as the distinctive story for Christians and points to a fall/redemption reality that defines our lives as followers of Christ. Central to this story is sin and the free gift of grace, which can only come through the cross. Jesus died for us. And we become worthy only through the bloody sacrifice of his broken body, and the humble sacrifice of our lives, serving in his name.

Women understand bloody sacrifice—whether it is the euphoric pain of birth, the solidarity we feel with the poor and the oppressed, or the perpetual sacrifice of putting ourselves last in the service of our families and our communities of faith. So the Christian narrative gives a context for our own lives and a deep spiritual connection to Jesus, whose sacrifice gives meaning to our own. But in the long tradition of the church, this exclusive focus on crucifixion, sin, pain, and sacrifice has been misused, and overused, to lock women into subservient and sacrificial roles that diminish the power and purpose of our vocational call in the world.

In my experience over the years, I have observed that women leaders embrace all three macrostories in Scripture—exodus and exile and resurrection—because our own stories find meaning in these biblical narratives. We know what it feels like to be enslaved by prescribed roles, to be enslaved by our own timidity and our own complicity with the power differentials of patriarchy. So with Miriam we rejoice in God's liberating power and God's captivating call. Like the exiled women weeping by the waters of Babylon, we also know what it feels like to be strangers in the strange land of a male-dominated culture. And the temptation we feel to be co-opted and assimilated into a male-defined culture is always there. Yes, we know what it feels like for the waters of fear to be parted. And through the opening of ordained offices of the church to women, we know what it feels like to come back home—out of exile—back home to the place of our spiritual birth. And so we are eager to lead God's people in a dance of life.

When it comes to the resurrection narrative, we women have discovered that the story of Jesus does not begin with the cross and the empty tomb. It begins with incarnation. And it is incarnation—God in the flesh—the very image of God implanted in Jesus—and the very image of God implanted in each one of us—that gives us the courage and the hope, the power and the promise to carry our crosses and endure the struggles of this world. God so loved the world that God became flesh and dwelt among us, easing our burdens, healing our brokenness, forgiving our sin, and carrying our suffering—not for us, but with us. And through the power of a risen and living Lord, the church—all of us—become the resurrected Body of Christ rejoicing and struggling with—and not for—the world God loves. We, both male and female, continue the work of incarnation—of God in flesh—carrying within our bodies and our souls the image of God.

Incarnational leadership is not solely practiced by women. But women have led the church to move in this direction in some pivotal ways. And central among them is the way we preach.

I'll never forget preaching on December 17, 1978. The lectionary text for the day was Luke 1:39–45, Mary's visit to Elizabeth. I was eight-and-a-half months pregnant at the time and had just that week made a pastoral visit to a woman who was equally "with child." We shared our anxieties about becoming mothers, our wonder at the workings of our bodies, our hopes for the children we were carrying. And the whole time, the babies in our wombs were leaping and kicking. That ordinary day, sitting at an ordinary kitchen table, the words of Scripture became flesh in the fabric of our daily lives. That was the first sermon I preached where incarnation became real to me. By telling Gods' story through my story, women and men were invited to experience incarnation in the stories of their own lives.

Narrative, metaphorical, imaginative preaching has long been the tradition of the church. And of course, it started with the homegrown parables and images in Jesus' teaching. But for too many years Reformed preaching was didactic expository preaching—three-point lectures aimed at capturing and transforming the mind. Thank God that we have discovered that God's word often sinks in best when it warms the heart and lifts the spirit and connects to the guts of everyday living. And women preachers and teachers have turned this kind of preaching into a fine art.

In the chapters of this book, personal stories, vulnerable confessions, and vivid images simply leap off the page—Joanna's Aunt Squeaky embodying grace in the sacristy of a Southern church; Deborah's portrait of Margaret Towner being "clothed with Christ" in a borrowed robe, a robe that we sisters collectively have managed to make our own; the intellectual feast, focusing on daily vocation, that Cynthia describes at her childhood family table; Roberta's discovery that prayer is physical delight and that faith is life "with" God and not "about" God; and Young Moon's gift to her daughter, a vivid rainbow blessing woven by God's tenacious covenant promise.

Much of women's preaching is invitation, not exhortation. It is vulnerable, not invincible. And it weaves a common fabric of human experience through feeling and story and metaphor. It is an incarnational experience—ingesting and chewing on the word so that it becomes flesh, getting up off the pages of the Bible and walking into the lives of the listeners, and then out into the life of the world. Preaching becomes light and salt and yeast—illumining and flavoring and leavening the faith, so that *ekklesia* can become a living Word, fleshy and fruitful in our Monday through Saturday living. And this incarnational Word often becomes incarnational sacrament, as we pour lavish amounts of water into the font and break the eucharistic bread with gusto, encouraging believers to touch and taste and see a God who washes us and feeds us with extravagant grace.

## Relational Leadership

Recently I had the privilege of serving as the keynote speaker at two women's conferences held at Mo-Ranch in Texas. As I flew into alien territory, I was anxious about how I, a northern "liberal," would fit into a southern, more conservative milieu. But I had forgotten how women do things. Hospitality and warmth and gracious welcome surrounded me for a week, and disagreements never eclipsed good manners. The most astonishing thing about the week was the way the leadership team connected. The twenty of us—directors and workshop conveners, worship leaders and speakers—bonded like a family, laughing and praying and sipping wine each evening, sharing the stories of our days, affirming each other's gifts, and collaboratively planning the next day's events. Every decision emerged out of consensus. No opinion was dismissed, and no idea was ignored. And every day the "chaplain" of the team put a gift on our pillow—candy or a prayer or an embroidered tea towel. It was like no other conference I have ever attended. The living Christ was vividly alive in our midst, not only in what we did but in how we did it.

Several chapters in this book refer to the foundational work of Carol Gilligan, the Harvard psychologist who published *In A Different Voice* in 1982.

Generalizations about all women are as dangerous as an artificial separation of men's style from women's style is false. But Gilligan's clarity about the developmental differences between men and women is significant, and her ideas underline for me the providential wisdom of our creative God.

Gilligan's developmental paradigm built around relationship speaks truth in the very marrow of my being. It is a lens that helps me understand the difference that women's visible leadership has made in the church. Though I tend to be assertive and verbal and forceful in my public leadership—qualities usually associated with men—the core convictions of my ministry are rooted in relationship—in collaboration, in weaving webs of connection in communities and decision-making bodies, in seeking consensus rather than majority rule whenever possible, in balancing the absolute truth of doctrine with the contextual reality of each situation, and in harmonizing policy with human story when shaping and applying personnel policies. And I have seen how this relational quality of women's leadership has begun to reshape polity and Presbyterian mission across this country.

In more and more presbyteries and congregations, emerging worship leadership—much of it female—is beginning to create worship experiences where use of the multiple intelligences and the five senses is helping to increase the participation level of worshipers. At the same time, art and drama and liturgical dance has added balance to the predominately rational and verbal ways of proclaiming the Word. In this way, liturgy becomes the relational work of the people and not just the idiosyncratic words of the preacher.

In councils and presbyteries led by women, community building, small-group discernment, and dialogue toward consensus building often replaces the efficiency and rigidity of parliamentary process. In visioning and planning efforts, grass roots involvement and common values and visions are replacing the top-down emphasis on goals and objectives. In my own clergy support group, the focus has changed since women have entered the group. Rather than trying to impress one another with our success stories, we are beginning to share our failures and our vulnerabilities, becoming friends instead of competitors in ministry. And for many women career advancement has come to mean not climbing the ladder but instead balancing all the relationships of our lives—family and friends as well as a community of Christ's people.

There is a downside to the relational reality of women's leadership within the church. The emphasis on the contextual nature of God's grace can often discount the demanding truth of the gospel. In being "nice," we sometimes cease to be faithful. This leads not only to relativism that waters down the costly grace of discipleship but also to a blurring of boundaries, where in trying to be everyone's friend we cease to be spiritual mentors, those who lead ourselves and others toward repentance and wholeness in the Christian faith. So once again we need the partnership and wisdom of our brothers in the faith to balance our ministries, as together we serve the whole people of God.


## Leading into the Future

In our twenty-first-century world, the North American Christian church is in crisis. The gospel vision of a just and generous church is at odds with the materialistic, high-tech, entertainment culture in which we live—a culture where immediate self-gratification supersedes love of neighbor and the intellectual heritage of the Reformed tradition simply fades in the high-octane emotion of a feel-good culture. In a polarized world, where conservatives and liberals glare at one another over chasms of hostility, the vision of the peaceable kindom seems naïve. Yet God's dream of shalom continues to be the breath of life that keeps hope alive. As the Presbyterian Church (U.S.A.) struggles to survive and thrive, the unique leadership gifts of women can help us become a new kind of church.


## Claiming the Vocation of Baptism

In the 1970s struggles to affirm the ordination of women, my favorite political button said it all: "ORDAIN WOMEN—OR STOP BAPTIZING THEM!" Baptism is the original "ordination" of us all—the total claim of God on our lives, the empowerment of the Holy Spirit for discipleship, the blessing that seals God's unconditional promise—the promise that nothing can separate us from the love of God. Baptism is the call into ministry for every man, woman, and child. And so the particular offices of the church become specific and functional ways to act out our baptisms—no more or less important than the vocations of ministry that church members act out day in and day out.

Women leaders within the church understand ministry to be more than the responsibilities listed in a position description. Marriage is ministry. Raising children is ministry. Caring for aging parents is ministry. Volunteering for the PTA is ministry. Marching in an anti-war protest is ministry. Folding laundry is ministry. Feeding the poor is ministry. This wholistic understanding of the Christian life as ministry empowers worshipers and lay leaders to understand their own lives as vocational gifts to God, and it focuses the worship and life of the church on equipping members to be God's image in the world in all aspects of work, family, and civic life. This font-based theology leads to a "high" doctrine of baptism—the identity that gives meaning to our lives—and a "low" doctrine of ordination—a functional way of giving shape to our baptismal identity. The result is an engagement and empowerment of the laity that equips the church to be "the provisional demonstration of what God intends for all of humanity."[2]

Such an affirmation of baptism as the common calling of all Christians leads to a hospitable understanding of the church—an openness to those normally left out—Letty Russell's "roundtable ministry" that generously welcomes the "least of these." Having been the victims of centuries of discrimination where our full baptismal vocation was denied, women leaders in the church are sensitized to those who are outsiders today. As the church is challenged by multicultural realities, growing immigrant populations, and worship styles and spiritual hungers that challenge our understandings of comfort, it is this common pool of baptismal grace that invites us to open our hearts and our minds. Having once been the strange ones excluded from the heart of Christian ministry, women have an instinctive solidarity with the strangers in our world today. For we know the joy that invitation and inclusion can bring. It does not surprise me that 85 percent of clergywomen within the PC(USA) are supportive of the ordination of our gay and lesbian brothers and sisters. God's extravagant grace includes us all.

In the congregation I serve, we begin every worship service by remembering our baptism. As I pour streams of water into our font in the very midst of the sanctuary, we are reminded of our common blessing and our common calling—to glorify God and enjoy God with the daily living of our lives.

## Patterns of Partnership

My current male colleague in ministry intentionally decided to seek an associate position as his first call out of seminary, and he intentionally looked for a congregation that was served by a female head of staff. It seemed to him, in looking around the church, that staff teams led by women were more collegial, less competitive, and more open to a diversity of gifts and opinions. Because of the relational dimension of adult female development, my colleague's unscientific assumption may indeed be true. Not only are women more inclined to be partners in ministry; women need partnerships in order to do quality ministry. And such a focus on horizontal instead of vertical dimensions of ministry more accurately reflects the divine image in our midst.

The very heart of Christian theology is the community of the Trinity, God's intrinsic nature of partnership and friendship. Jesus gathered a team of twelve around him and found nourishment for his soul in small communities of friends. Egalitarian table fellowship was the focal point of his ministry, and empowering the faith and gifts of those around him occupied much of his time. It seems that collaboration and community is the gospel's answer to division and despair within the church, and more often than not women leaders are setting more places at the table instead of locking the doors of the church.

## Serving as Ambassadors of Reconciliation

Whether it is violence in the home, violence in the church, or violence in the world, these modern days are filled with brokenness and division. The vision of shalom seems like the far-distant fantasy of an out-of-touch God. But those of us baptized into Christ have been given a gift and a promise, for Christ has come to break down the dividing walls of hostility, to inaugurate a reign of peace and justice for all God's children. Jim Wallis suggests that we Christians continually need to ask God's question: "How are the children doing?"[3] We women, who have physically and spiritually birthed and nurtured the children of this world, instinctively carry that question in our souls. The only answer that makes sense is the answer Jesus gives: "Let the little children come to me, and do not stop them; for it is to such as these that the kingdom of God belongs. . . . And he took them up into his arms, laid his hands on them, and blessed them" (Mark 10:14–16).

If the church is going to survive, if the Middle East is going to survive, if the political fabric of this nation is going to survive, we need to stop the dividing and start the healing. We need to turn difference into diversity, argument into dialogue, enmity into hospitality, truth bashing into grace giving. We need to embrace the Christian vocation as described by Paul—to be ambassadors of reconciliation—a new creation—serving in Christ's name. The ancient challenge offered to Esther is the same challenge confronting the women of today. For such a time as this, God has called and empowered women within the Presbyterian Church (U.S.A.) to model a new way of being church. And we dare not let God down.

## Blessed to Be a Blessing

In her wonderful book, *My Grandfather's Blessings*, Rachel Naomi Remen, M.D. tells the story of her childhood. She was the daughter of two busy professionals who worshiped work rather than God. Every Friday afternoon,

Naomi would go and visit her grandfather, who was a rabbi. They would drink tea; he would tell her the wonderful stories of the Jewish tradition; and then he would bless her. He would lay his hands upon her head, as every Jewish parent does for every child each Sabbath day. And he would name her again and again—Neshume-le—"beloved little soul."

One day her grandfather explained to Rachel the meaning of a minyan— the group of ten men within the orthodox Jewish tradition who are needed to create "a portable Temple" to become, together, a place where the Holy can reside. Naomi couldn't understand why ten women could not also form a minyan. Sadly, her grandfather would respond, "Because it is the law."[4]

A few years later, as the old man lay dying, he called for young Naomi to come to his side. He took her hand. And with quivering voice he blessed her one more time: "Neshume-le, you are a *minyan* all by yourself."[5]

During the last hundred years the church has slowly invited women into the *minyan* of ministry, blessing us through the touch of ordination and acknowledging the presence of God in the gifts of every person's life.

On the September afternoon thirty years ago when I knelt in the chancel of that Boston church for the laying of hands, all I felt was the pressure and the burden of an uncertain future. Later, when I left the sanctuary to go home, cold rain was falling from a dark sky. But then, when I looked up, I saw the blessing. There, stretched across the clouds, was a perfect rainbow, and I was reminded that the call of ministry is not about me. It is about the providence of a gracious God who calls us and sends us, sin and all.

Thanks be to God. Amen.

# Acknowledgments

Extracts from Carol J. Schlueter, "Feminist Homiletics: Strategies for Empowerment," in *Women's Visions: Theological Reflection, Celebration, Action*, ed. Ofelia Ortega (Geneva: World Council of Churches Publications, 1995), 138. Used by permission of WCC Publications.

# Notes

CHAPTER 1: "NOW IS THE TIME!"

1. As I remember it but not her exact words.

CHAPTER 3: WEARING THE ROBE

1. Margaret Gibson Hummel and Mildred Roe, *The Amazing Heritage*, (Philadelphia: Geneva Press, 1970), 71–72.

2. *The Constitution of the Presbyterian Church (U.S.A.)*, Part II, *Book of Order* (Louisville, KY: Office of the General Assembly, Presbyterian Church (U.S.A.), 1999), G-60202a.

3. "A First Lady Minister in Robes of a New Role," *Life* 41, no. 20 (Nov 12, 1956): 151.

4. Information from personal conversation with Margaret Towner in 2005.

5. Brief Statement of Faith, *The Constitution of the Presbyterian Church (U.S.A.)*, Part I, *Book of Confessions* (Louisville, KY: Office of the General Assembly, Presbyterian Church (U.S.A.), 1999).

CHAPTER 6: FROM THE KITCHEN TO THE PULPIT

1. "Here I Am, Lord" *The Presbyterian Hymnal: Hymns, Psalms, and Spiritual Songs* (Louisville, KY: Westminster/John Knox Press, 1990), 525.

2. During the Korean War, many Christians in North Korea came to the south seeking freedom of faith and still miss their homeland.

3. *Hahb-Dong* literally means "union." Presbyterian churches are the biggest denominations in Korea, having more than six million members.

4. The Presbyterian Church in the Republic of Korea passed the overture of women's ordination at General Assembly in 1974; there are about 160 ordained women pastors. The Presbyterian Church of Korea did in 1994, currently having about 420 ordained women pastors.

5. Jay R. Greenberg and Stephen A. Mitchell, *Object Relations in Psychoanalytic Theory* (Cambridge, MA: Harvard University Press, 1983)

6. Carol Gilligan, *In A Different Voice* (Cambridge, MA: Harvard University Press, 1982); Rosemary Chinnici, *Can Women Re-image the Church?* (Mahwah, NJ: Paulist Press, 1992).

7. It literally means "evangelist." However, a student intern is usually called *Jun-Do-Sa-Nim* in Korean churches. While a male *Jun-Do-Sa-Nim* would become a pastor, a female *Jun-Do-Sa-Nim* is usually a permanent title for a nonordained woman minister.

8. See Judith Berling's article "Confucianism," written for the Asia Society's *Focus on Asian Studies* 2, no. 1 *Asian Religions*, (Fall 1982): 5–7.

9. Although it was a small gathering at that time, it has become larger. Currently, there are about sixty ordained Korean women pastors in PC(USA).

10. *Shimtuh* literally means "resting place."

11. Words and Music by Carolyn McDade, copyright © 1984, Surtsey Publishing; used by permission.

12. There are about 1.5 million Korean Americans. The history of Korean immigrants to the United States goes back to1903 in Hawaii as sugar-cane plantation workers; the big wave of immigration took place since mid-1970s. About 75 percent of Korean Americans claim themselves as Christian. There are about 400 churches and about 50,000 church members belonging to PC(USA).

13. First generation consists of those born and raised in Korea, and second generation are those who were born and raised in the United States. Between them, there is a 1.5 generation consisting of those born in Korea and raised in the United States.

14. Korean Americans as a minority are struggling with racial discrimination, the "middle-agent minority" phenomenon, and classism. Andrew Sung Park, *Racial Conflict and Healing: An Asian-American Theological Perspective* (Maryknoll, NY: Orbis Books, 1996), 26–40.

15. Patricia Mei Yin Chang, "Female Clergy in the Contemporary Protestant Church: A Current Assessment," *Journal for the Scientific Study of Religion* 36, no. 4 (1997): 568.

16. Ibid., 569.

17. Ibid., 567.

18. Ibid., 569.

## CHAPTER 7: HEADLINES OF THE STRUGGLE

1. Throughout the Presbyterian Church's various manifestations in this country, the form of government has remained consistent. Congregations elect and ordain deacons and elders, and they elect pastors with the approval of the presbytery, which ordains them. *The Constitution* of the Presbyterian Church (U.S.A.) includes the *Book of Order*, where one finds the *Form of Government* that contains the requirements for ordination. Amendments to the *Book of Order* occur when a General Assembly and a majority of the presbyteries vote to approve them.

2. *Minutes of the General Assembly,* Presbyterian Church in the United States of America, An Appendix, 1832, 348.

3. Lois A. Boyd and R. Douglas Brackenridge, *Presbyterian Women in America, Two Centuries of a Quest for Status*, 2nd ed. (Westport, CT: Greenwood Press, 1996), 96.

4. Ibid., 98.

5. Ibid.

6. Annie E. K. Bidwell and Dorothy J. Hill, ed., *Rancho Chico Indians* (Chico, CA: Bidwell Mansion Association, 1987), 49–51.

7. Lois H. McDonald, *Annie Kennedy Bidwell, An Intimate History* (Chico, CA: Stansbury Publication, 2004), 151.

8. *Minutes of the Twentieth General Assembly*, United Presbyterian Church of North America, 1878, 568.

9. Boyd and Brackenridge, *Presbyterian Women in America, Two Centuries of a Quest for Status,* 1st ed. (Westport, CT: Greenwood Press, 1983) 111.

10. Boyd and Brackenridge, *Presbyterian Women*, 2nd ed., 134.

11. Ibid., 124–25.

12. Ibid., 113, 118.

13. Jean Huffman, "Ten Women Who Made A Difference, Louisa M. Woosley," *Concern,* April 1987, 39–40.

14. Boyd and Brackenridge, *Presbyterian Women,* 1st ed., 120.

15. Ibid., 120.

16. George P. Donehoo, "Feminism in the Church," *The Presbyterian,* January 20, 1921, 26.

17. ———, "Editorial: The Report on the Committee on Ordination of Women," *The Presbyterian,* May 1920, 2.

18. *Minutes of the General Assembly,* The Presbyterian Church in the United States of America, Journal Report and Statistics, 1921, 44.

19. Margaret Gibson Hummel, and Mildred Roe, *The Amazing Heritage* (Philadelphia: Geneva Press, 1970), 138.

20. Ibid., 139.

21. Margaret E. Hodge, M. Katharine Bennett, "Causes of Unrest Among Women of the Church," General Council of the Presbyterian Church in the U.S.A., November 30, 1927, 10.

22. M. Katherine (sic) Bennett, Margaret Hodge, "Overtures on Women Now Before the Church, An Open Letter to Women in the Presbyterian Church in the U.S.A.," *The Presbyterian Banner,* October 8, 1929, 27.

23. M. Katharine Bennett, "Those Restless Women," *The Presbyterian Banner,* April 18, 1929, 13.

24. Ibid., 13.

25. Boyd and Brackenridge, *Presbyterian Women,* 2nd ed., 119.

26. Ibid., 121.

27. Ibid., 123.

28. Ibid., 125.

29. Boyd and Brackenridge, *Presbyterian Women,* 1st ed., 145.

30. Ibid., 145.

31. Mildred Roe, "A Gift Was Given," *Outreach,* August-September, 1947, 196.

32. Boyd and Brackenridge, *Presbyterian Women,* 1st ed., 146.

33. Boyd and Brackenridge, *Presbyterian Women,* 2nd ed., 128.

34. Ibid.

35. Ibid.

36. Margaret E. Towner, "Ordained to the Gospel Ministry," *Concern,* January 1981, 4.

37. Boyd and Brackenridge, *Presbyterian Women,* 1st ed., 105.

38. Ibid., 105, 109.

39. Ibid., 109.

40. Ibid., 213.

41. Ibid., 213.

42. Boyd and Brackenridge, *Presbyterian Women,* 2nd ed., 130.

43. Minutes of the One-Hundred Third General Assembly of the Presbyterian Church in the United States, April 25–30, 1963, 108.

44. Minutes of the One-Hundred Fourth General Assembly of the Presbyterian Church in the United States, April 23–28, 1964, 110.

45. Louise H. Farrior, *Journey Toward the Future* (Atlanta: Women's Office of Presbyterian Church (U.S.), 1986), 129.

46. Ibid.

## CHAPTER 8: FROM THE BAPTISMAL FONT INTO A LIFE OF SERVICE

1. Paul Tillich, *Systematic Theology,* vol. 3 (Chicago: University of Chicago Press, 1963), 212–13.

2. See especially William L. Andrews, ed. *Sisters of the Spirit* (Bloomington: Indiana University Press, 1986); Henry Louis Gates Jr. *Slave Narratives* (New York: Oxford University Press, 1988).

## CHAPTER 11: ENCOUNTERS AND VISIONS

1. Bärbel von Wartenberg-Potter, *We Will Not Hang Our Harps on the Willows*, Risk Series, (Geneva: World Council of Churches Publications, 1987), 29.

2. Leonardo Boff, *Way of the Cross, Way of Justice* (Maryknoll, NY: Orbis Books, 1982), 48.

3. John W. De Gruchy, *Cry Justice! Prayers, Meditations and Readings from South Africa* (Maryknoll, NY: Orbis Books, 1986), 25.

4. The metaphor used by Dr. Letty M. Russell in her book *Church in the Round: Feminist Interpretation of the Church* (Louisville, KY: Westminster/John Knox Press, 1993) helped us to better understand this concept of "open Church" or "the church in its surroundings."

5. Joann Wolski Conn, ed., *Women's Spirituality* (New York: Paulist Press, 1986), 14.

6. *Alive Together: A Practical Guide to Ecumenical Learning* (Geneva: Education Sub-Unit, World Council of Churches, 1989), 7.

7. Letty M. Russell, "Ecumenical Learning in Theological Education: A Woman's Perspective," in *God Has Called Us*, ed. Lynda Katsuno, Kathy Keay, and Ofelia Ortega (Geneva: World Council of Churches, 1994), 37.

8. Ibid., 38.

9. Carol J. Schlueter, "Feminist Homiletics: Strategies for Empowerment," in *Women's Visions: Theological Reflection, Celebration, Action,* ed. Ofelia Ortega (Geneva: World Council of Churches, 1995), 138.

10. Ortega, ed., *Women's Visions*, 177.

## CHAPTER 13: OUTSIDERS WITHIN

1. Material on "Outsider Within" was first used by me on a panel entitled "Outsiders Within: Feminism within Religious and Ecumenical Institutions," at a Conference on Religion and the Feminist Movement held at Harvard Divinity School, Nov. 2, 2002.

2. Elizabeth Howell Verdesi, *In But Still Out: Women in the Church* (Philadelphia: Westminster Press, 1976).

3. Letty M. Russell, *Human Liberation in a Feminist Perspective—A Theology* (Philadelphia: Westminster Press, 1974).

4. Cf. Beverly Wildung Harrison, "Feminist Thea(o)logies in the Millennium," in *Liberating Eschatology: Essays in Honor of Letty M. Russell*, ed., Margaret A. Farley and Serene Jones (Louisville, KY: Westminster John Knox Press, 1999), 156–71.

5. Letty M. Russell, Kwok, Pui-lan, Ada Maria Isasi-Diaz, and Katie Geneva Cannon, eds., *Inheriting Our Mothers' Gardens: Feminist Theology in Third World Perspective* (Philadelphia: Westminster Press, 1988).

6. Although women have long struggled against their subordination in the United States, the first movement for liberation arose out of the abolitionist struggle against slavery and continued until women's suffrage was gained in the early twentieth-century. The second women's

movement arose in the late 1960s following the civil rights and antiwar movements and continues in many different forms.

7. J. C. Hoekendijk, *The Church Inside Out*, ed. by L. A. Hoedemaker and Pieter Tijmes (Philadelphia: Westminster Press, 1966).

8. Letty M. Russell, *Church in the Round: Feminist Interpretation of the Church* (Louisville, KY: Westminster John Knox Press, 1993), 124.

9. Russell, *Church in the Round,* 14. See also Paul D. Hanson, *The People Called: The Growth of Community in the Bible* (San Francisco: Harper & Row, 1986).

10. Letty M. Russell, "Women and Unity; Problem or Possibility?" *Mid-Stream: An Ecumenical Journal* 21, no. 3 (July, 1982): 298–304.

11. Christine D. Pohl, *Making Room: Recovering Hospitality as a Christian Tradition* (Grand Rapids: Wm. B. Eerdmans Publishing Co., 1999), 3.

12. Russell, *Church in the Round*, 173.

13. Henri Nouwen, *Reaching Out: The Three Movements of the Spiritual Life* (New York: Doubleday, 1975), 79–81.

14. Information on the Circle of Concerned African Women Theologians is available on the Web at http://www.thecirclecawt.org/.

## CHAPTER 14: THANKS BE TO GOD!

1. Marcus Borg, *Meeting Jesus Again for the First Time* (San Francisco: HarperSanFrancisco, 1994), chap. 6.

2. *Constitution of the Presbyterian Church (U.S.A.)*, Part 1, *Book of Order* (Louisville, KY: Office of the General Assembly, Presbyterian Church (U.S.A.), ), G3.0200.

3. Jim Wallis, *God's Politics* (San Francisco: HarperSanFrancisco, 2005), 29.

4. Rachel Naomi Remen, *My Grandfather's Blessing* (New York: Riverhead Books, 2000), 22.

5. Ibid., 364.